ENTERPRISE WITHIN™

Developing corporate enterprise and innovation through stretchy staff

Rebecca Jones

Enjoy
Rebecca
x

This edition was first published in 2017

Copyright © 2017 Rebecca Jones
Published by Red Shoe Business Press
Illustrations © 2017 Rebecca Jones

ISBN: 978-0-993-38043-3

The rights of Rebecca Jones to be identified as the author of this work have been asserted by her in accordance with the Copyright, Designs and Patents Act 1988.

A CIP record of this book is available from the British Library.

All rights reserved. No part of this book may be reproduced, stored in a retrieval system, or transmitted in any form or by any means, electronic, mechanical, photocopying, recording or otherwise, without the prior written permission of the copyright holder.

No responsibility for loss occasioned to any person acting or refraining from action as a result of any material in this publication can be accepted by the author or publisher.

A big thanks to my clients,
who have tried out the ideas held within the book.
To my family, for their understanding of my desire
to make this book come to life.

Importantly, thanks to those who have given me the
encouragement to make it happen and the patience to
read, review, check, and advise.

You all know who you are.
Thanks to each and every one of you.

*It takes a village to bring up a child;
it takes a community of supportive peers
to publish a book!*

Contents

About the Author	6
Early Reader Reviews	8
Introduction	11
Why This Book?	16

PART ONE: You Should Embrace Enterprise Within™

Chapter 1 – Embrace Enterprise in Your Organisation	19

PART TWO: What Is Enterprise Within™?

Chapter 2 – Enterprise Within: the Process	41

PART THREE: How to Embed Enterprise Within™ in Your Organisation

Chapter 3 – Enterprise Needs Structure to Be Flexible	65
Chapter 4 – Future-proof Your Organisation with Staff Engagement and Enterprise	77
Chapter 5 – Multi-level Communication – Joining up the Dots	93
Chapter 6 - Customer-led Growth – More than Just What People Want	105

PART FOUR: Enabling Enterprise Within™ in Your Organisation

Chapter 7 – Learning Ladder to Growth	119
Chapter 8 – Generating and Developing Enterprise Ideas	137
Chapter 9 – Developing an Enterprise Project – It's All in the Planning	157
Chapter 10 – Supporting and Managing Enterprising Staff	167
Final Words from the Author	187
Moving Forward...	189
Further Reading	191

About the Author

Rebecca Jones started her first business at the age of 19 and has since established herself within the field of business growth and staff engagement. She holds various qualifications in enterprise and education and has researched enterprise learning for the last 17 years. She has combined running her own training business for over two decades with owning a guest house and working in academia and people development. She has taught at several business schools on enterprise programs from business start-ups to a Master's in Mentoring Entrepreneurs.

Rebecca uses her knowledge of people development and business growth to provide an interesting blend of thinking and ideas when it comes to achieving business success — particularly focused on the idea: "Can your staff be more enterprising to help your organisation grow?"

Rebecca works with banks, national companies, not-for-profit organisations, independent schools, small and large companies, government bodies, and universities to establish a more enterprising approach. She connects enterprise with engaging staff, listening to customer needs, and building sustainable approaches to organisational growth and stability.

Rebecca has developed her work with clients to blend staff engagement and business development. Whilst working in various companies, she discovered that staff feel disconnected from the development of an organisation when they have little or no knowledge of how the organisation runs and how enterprise is successful.

Rebecca has worked with clients who wish their staff were more involved in their organisation. She is often brought in to encourage and support business development as well as staff engagement. This work has led to the development of her own approach "Enterprise Within™" and so to this book.

Early Reader Reviews

"In a business environment where markets can emerge and disappear almost overnight, growth can be exponential or muted, and customer choice is vast in terms of product or channel, the organisations that adapt will be the ones that survive, and having employees who have an agile mind-set and broad capabilities will enable this. This book helps employers identify the right talent and traits and use them mutually and effectively. Thought-provoking and practical."

*— Donna Trapnell,
Director, Banking Operations*

"A compelling read for anyone who wants to expand their awareness and find constructive guidance on how to embed an enterprise mind-set into their organisation."

*— Christine Marsh CPT,
Business Relationships Expert & International Speaker*

"Aligning your people to your organisation and realising the potential in both is essential to any organisation's success. This book gives you the opportunity to engage and empower with its unique and refreshing "enterprise within" approach. A must-read book!"

*— Julian John,
MD Delsion HR & Disability Inclusion Consultancy*

"Whilst on the surface this book is about enterprise, there are some great internal communications lessons here for people in all sorts of organisations of all sizes and sectors."

— *Gwyn Williams,*
Director of Communications, S4C.

"In this book, Rebecca has developed a route map for established leaders and those new to role to steer their teams into this new normality of having 'stretchy staff' — staff who actively seek solutions and new opportunities that are outside their comfort zone for the good of the bottom line and improved service delivery. A culture of enterprise is no longer the preserve of 'business development teams', but rather needs to feature in the DNA of the whole organisation."

— *Aled Davies,*
Retired Chief Superintendent

"If you are running a business, or are involved in running a business, this is a book you need right alongside you and you need to regularly address the questions it asks. I do believe that no business will win in the future without an enterprise mind-set throughout the organisation, with employee-led initiatives and ' stretchy' people and this book gives you THE tools to get you on that journey."

— *Roger Harrop,*
The CEO Expert

"A clearly written, practical book that leaves the reader in no doubt how valuable an enterprising mind-set is to all businesses. Enterprise Within offers a system to develop individuals, teams, and ultimately the organisation to become stronger and more effective. An excellent manual for leaders and employees."

– Dr Lynda Shaw,
Neuroscientist and Business Psychologist

"Developing staff and helping them reach their full potential is at the heart of any successful business large or small. Rebecca Jones gives you first-hand insight into how identifying, fostering, and facilitating enterprising staff can help you realise the potential of your business. If you want to realise the potential of your business, then this book is an excellent starting point. Clear, concise, and thought-provoking this is a must-read for anybody wanting to develop an enterprising workforce."

– Prof Gary Packham,
Pro Vice Chancellor (Innovation and Entrepreneurship),
Anglia Ruskin University.

"Rebecca Jones has established a route map, enabling business leaders to empower their steams to enhance business performance. In a world where competitive advantage is harder to come by, ensuring the maximum utilisation of an organisations talent pool is increasingly important."

– Mike Davies,
Head of Public Sector Banking, UK High Street Bank

Introduction

Let's face it, more and more senior staff within organisations are being asked to take responsibility for business growth. At the same time, they need to find new income streams whilst being more customer-focused. Doing more with less is becoming a basic requirement. It's likely that at this very moment, you and your team are looking for innovative ideas—ways of increasing profits and staying ahead of your competitors. Everyone is being asked to come up with ideas, to be *enterprising*.

Organisations often know that it is their staff who can make the difference. It is your employees who can now make the difference at a deeper level—from improving customer service to new product development. Various techniques have been used in the past to encourage staff to give their best and be more engaged, from rewards-based ideas to the risk of consequence. But these carrot-and-stick options are now outdated. The concept of telling your staff "if you do something good, you get extra money and if you don't, you will lose money, privileges, or your job" is unlikely to build relationships based on respect and inspire people to do their best.

Staff need to feel proud of that they do, who they work for, and the services or products they provide. Only when they are proud can they really become connected and engaged with their employers. Encouraging enterprise in an organisation provides opportunities for higher levels of staff enjoyment: a feeling of being involved in the solutions and being able to impact on the quality of the organisation moving forward. This can lead to staff feeling prouder and willing to work harder for their employers.

Organisations need to improve staff engagement to drive diversity of thought, which can lead to new and improved ideas that enable you to remain relevant to customer needs in a fast, changing world. You need to enable a more enterprising mind-set within your employees. This means empowering employees to stretch outside their comfort zones and to make decisions for themselves — decisions that give customers the best experience possible and provide the solutions to build a sustainable organisation. Staff must feel able to implement ideas without fear of consequence.

By creating a more enterprising way of working across the whole organisation, staff will grow and move on to new, more challenging experiences. Ideas will be developed, incubated, and flourish in a supportive environment. In short, enterprise provides opportunities for individuals and the whole organisation to grow. Embracing a culture that is continuously learning and evolving drives advocacy and ensures staff see enterprise as a natural activity they should take part in.

This book demonstrates the theory of encouraging staff involvement in enterprise as a way to improve staff engagement. This way of working not only helps to improve an individual's connection to the organisation, but also increases their confidence in their skills and helps them feel more empowered and valued. Organisations who implement these tools and ideas effectively can expect to see greater performance levels, organisational growth, and lower staff turnover.

If you are looking to the future as a manager or leader, then you will need to embrace a culture of enterprise to be successful. If you are yet to be a manager or leader but wish to follow that path, then understanding enterprise within a company will help you stand out from the rest. The traditional belief that enterprise is risky needs to be quashed for leaders to feel able to relinquish some level of control to their employees — this book will show you how to do that.

If your organisation has concerns about its long-term future, then enabling enterprise is the answer. For organisations who face uncertain times, it may be because they are no longer profitable, or because they are delivering goods and services in a way that people no longer wish to receive. Outdated practices, poor performance, you name it. Being more enterprising is an option to resolve a range of difficulties. If your organisation is already doing very well, then by adding enterprise into the mix, you will only become a stronger and better performing organisation overall.

This book demonstrates how you can implement the Enterprise Within™ system in your organisation.

What is the Enterprise Within™ system?

More and more staff within organisations are being asked to find income streams, and be more enterprising and customer-focused. The system they use to do this takes the concept of enterprise learning and places it within the structure of an organisation. At the same time, it is wrapped around other tools that enable it to become embedded in the culture of the organisation.

Using enterprise as a tool to develop and encourage growth and quality within your organisation is not a just way of making money. It is a way of connecting the needs of your clients or service users with the ability of your employees to meet those needs. It is about business development, with a sprinkle of innovation and an eye on customer need and staff engagement. This system has become "Enterprise Within™". Delivered as in-house courses, talks, and workshops, it has now been written for you in this book.

The Enterprise Within™ system covers the following core areas, which will be covered in the book:

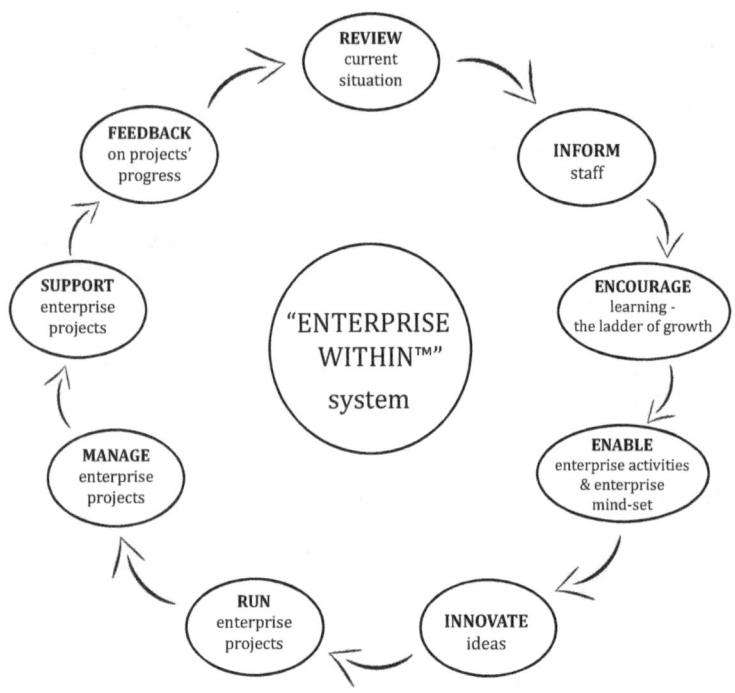

What are "stretchy staff"?

Staff are so important to the success of an organisation. Their willingness to develop themselves and the organisation they work for often comes down to good will, personal motivation, and an understanding of how to spot opportunities and make change happen. For far too long, we have asked staff members to be flexible. But for me, flexibility is about slightly flexing or shifting from the current position, not making the larger changes we now need to keep up to date with current, increasing demands. To ensure that organisations experience the exponential growth needed to survive, we need more than the previous small gains produced by enabling flexibility in your workforce. If your organisation needs more than a small shift, then you need to ask your staff not to be flexible—but to be *stretchy*.

Think about it, flexibility is about altering your working hours, or being willing to take on a slightly different way of working that's flexible. I believe that to embrace change and develop a more enterprising way of working, staff need to look at things from a different perspective, step outside their comfort zone, and consider things in a way they may have never done before.

Stretchy staff will take on new tasks knowing that in order to do so, they have to learn new skills they don't currently possess. They will have to take on challenges that they don't feel comfortable with. However, they do all this accepting that when we stretch ourselves, we need to grow and develop. They do this knowing that it will take effort and that they might need support to do so. They also realise that sometimes, things won't go to plan so adjustments will need to be made and ideas will need to be retried. To be stretchy, we need to embrace an approach of accepting that we must try and not being afraid of failing, as it as part of the process of developing.

Why This Book?

This book is the culmination of my work with organisations to embrace "Enterprise Within™" and it provides you with the information to do the same.

An increasing number of companies are now encouraging their staff to take on an enterprising mind-set. This book will inspire you and your team whilst giving you the tools to consider a new approach to organisational growth.

What this book will demonstrate

- Why you need to embrace a culture of enterprise
- How your staff are the answer to organisational growth
- The tools required to ensure that enterprise happens in your organisation.

Who this book is for

Leaders, executives, company owners, and senior managers of organisations who feel they need to develop a culture of enterprise to enable their organisations to grow and be stable for the future.

How to read this book

The first chapter is about why you should change and what the benefits are. You can cover this quickly.

The second chapter then outlines the Enterprise Within™ system and how you can develop and embed enterprise in your organisation in order to increase performance, profits, and staff engagement.

The book will then delve deeper into the elements of the Enterprise Within™ system that enable enterprise to take place in your organisation and embed it to ensure future growth.

PART ONE:

Why You Should Embrace Enterprise Within™

"Embracing enterprise leads to organisational growth"

Chapter 1 –

Embrace Enterprise in Your Organisation

Enterprise isn't just something entrepreneurs do alone at their own risk – it's something we can all do to improve things for the future.

If you lead an organisation or have a role to play in the development of an organisation, you may find it difficult to keep coming up with new ideas and approaches. More than likely, you already know that to keep an organisation thriving and growing, it takes more than one good idea. But where can you get the next idea from? Well, have you considered your staff?

Getting your staff to engage more and find new ideas for you frees up your time to fully focus on delivering the best possible solutions to move your organisation forward. With the right skills and confidence, staff will embrace a more enterprising way of working.

This chapter will cover:

- What we mean by enterprise
- Can anyone be enterprising?
- What is an enterprise mind-set?
- Why you should embrace enterprise
- Frequently asked questions about enterprise and entrepreneurship within organisations

What is enterprise?

The word "enterprise" is often used to describe a business. In its original form, it comes from the French word *entreprendre*, meaning to undertake or *take in hand*. In this instance, enterprise is used to describe a new project or idea. Then, the new project or idea requires energy and enthusiasm to improve it, develop it, and drive it forward.

In the context of this book, "enterprise" is any activity or project, of any size, that can benefit the organisation. The aim of such activities are for an organisation to increase its profits; become more stable; rely less on loans, grants, or funding; and grow into a more sustainable business. Usually, this is done by creating something new or altering what you have, taking it in hand to ensure better quality, or offering a more profitable solution.

Enterprise is about being aware of things you can do to benefit the organisation you work for. This includes everything from resolving day-to-day issues to spotting opportunities to adding value to the organisation. It's about being ready to take on a challenge where it may be difficult to find a solution, but doing so with imaginativeness and willingness to embrace it, and giving it a try in order to improve.

Let's be clear: this is not about entrepreneurs

Entrepreneurs are individuals who see an opportunity or develop an idea, and with trial and error, hard graft, risk, and many sleepless nights, they turn it into a profitable business venture. They have a variety of skills and traits, but are most commonly considered to be self-starters and ambitious. Entrepreneurs on the whole carry out enterprising activities for their own gain, at their own risk.

However, not everyone who is enterprising does so for themselves. Enterprising individuals may have many of the same traits as an entrepreneur, but wish to carry out enterprising activities while still having the benefits of being employed. Within an established organisation, there may be enterprising staff, but they are not strictly entrepreneurs.

So are enterprising people really just entrepreneurs?

No, not fully. The traits of an entrepreneur are somewhat different to those of an enterprising person within an organisation. However, they do share some similarities such as willingness to champion their idea, taking charge of making it happen, and finding a way to make something happen when it seems unlikely to proceed.

Enterprising people often see things from a different perspective, are able to help others see opportunities, and can identify problems that an organisation never knew they had. They are individuals who are active and to some degree willing to take a risk. However, this risk may be more to their personal reputation rather than a risk to the organisation they work for. They see progress as something positive, not a risk to the status quo.

Will enterprising staff leave and set up their own business?

Don't worry about this. Whilst enterprising staff are often innovators, able to generate ideas and find solutions, they definitely prefer the safety of a paid position. There are many people in the world who have enterprising traits who do not want to do it for themselves. This can be because they don't have the willingness to risk their reputation and/or salaried position. Or because they don't feel they have the complete set of skills to go it alone. Possibly, they fear the unpredictability of being an entrepreneur, leader, or CEO.

By enabling staff to use their enterprising skills and enjoy their work, they are less likely to leave. However, be aware that if you do not support them in their work, they could look elsewhere for opportunities to use their enterprise mind-set.

The question should be "Do you want staff who have the ability to innovate working for you? Or are you happy for them to leave and work for your competitors or start up their own business and go into competition with you?"

What makes a good enterprising person?

Enterprising people are proactive and self-motivated, with a willingness to take action or start something. Their characteristics usually include: using their own initiative, being able to think differently, being willing to accept responsibility for taking considered risks, and being a leader of others, although not necessarily being in a leadership role. They also accept that they are operating within the necessary constraints and rules of an organisation.

They tend to be glass half-full rather than half-empty people. They are also willing to accept that they do not and will never know everything. This leads them to be collaborative people who work with others to seek out solutions.

Not every employee can be enterprising, however it will help you immensely if you can spot people with particular behaviours. Look through this list, think about your employees, and consider how many of these traits are already being demonstrated.

Someone who is enterprising would be seen as...	Number of staff I think have each trait
a builder of relationships	
someone with a "can do" attitude	

a generator of change	
a problem-solver	
opportunistic	
flexible	
willing to try and learn as they go	
enthusiastic	
independent and self-reliant	
someone with a stretchy mind-set	
engaged in the organisation	
capable and willing to make a difference	
solutions-focused	
resourceful	
self-motivated	
self-confident	
persistent	
able to turn ideas into reality	
willing to commit	
future-focused	
willing to enthuse others	
innovative	
a provider of customer satisfaction	
inquisitive about things	
someone who has an enterprise mind-set	

People with an enterprise mind-set exhibit a mix of behaviours, attributes, attitudes, competencies, and skills, and they are able to access resources and develop ideas.

Looking at this list, it is easy to see that many current staff already have a selection of these skills and therefore could become enterprising with some support and encouragement.

It is not necessary for one person to have all of these traits. Indeed, the concept of enterprise within an organisation is that by bringing several people together who have a range of traits and experiences, it creates a diversity of thought that provides a stronger base when developing enterprising projects. It is unlikely that anyone will have no suitable skills, but they may require support to identify these.

> ### Developing stretchy staff
>
> Encouraging your team members to be stretchy in the way they think about themselves and their skills can be the difference between them saying "I'm not enterprising" to saying "I think I could be enterprising".
>
> Think of it like this. A staff member believes that because they haven't done something before in exactly the way you are asking them to, then they don't have the skills and abilities needed. They're not considering skills in a stretchy way. For example, if you ask them to organise an event to promote a new project at work, they might think "I haven't done that before so I don't know whether I can" at first. However, you can encourage them to think of similar things they have done and link those in.
>
> So, if they start to think in a stretchy way, they can think of it as, "I have organised birthday parties before" or "I have some great social media skills I could use". While new areas they have no experience of might be harder, they just need to give it a try and stretch themselves. It's likely that they will surprise themselves with their new skills.

It's likely that you already know some of your enterprising staff. People who are naturally enterprising often come to the fore. They demonstrate their abilities through their actions, often initiating and developing projects for themselves. Instead of waiting for things to happen to them, they are willing to take action and if need be, take control. Importantly, such people are also willing to be held accountable, as their thought processes and decision-making are invariably rational and considered. Inside, they have an enterprise mind-set that sets them apart.

Enterprise mind-set

Whilst many people may see a need to resolve a problem or improve the way the organisation functions, not everyone believes they should do something about it, or are willing to take action. Sometimes in an organisation, we have staff who aren't even aware of problems, but that's a whole other book. For now, let's concentrate on staff who *can* identify a need.

What you need as a leader is staff who see that something is wrong, needs improving, or can identify an opportunity for the organisation. Then you need to support and encourage them to take action. What you don't want is staff members who tell you there is a problem and then you have to fix it. You need staff members who feel empowered and able to consider solutions and ideas, develop them, and bring them to your attention.

An enterprise mind-set is the commitment to achieving something that will enable a balance between a successful organisation and meeting the needs of customers by keeping an eye on the present and the future. It is made up of three elements:

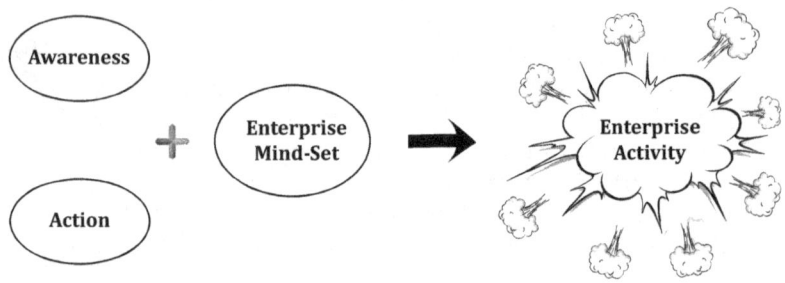

A person with an enterprise mind-set is open to seeing opportunities and ideas (awareness). They are then keen and able to review options, develop ideas, and bring those ideas to the table (action). They believe they can make this happen, know that they are not perfect and don't know everything, but are willing to give it a try and believe that with support and effort, they could achieve it (mind-set).

Awareness

This means seeing opportunities around you, such as the needs and changing needs of customers and clients. It means keeping an eye on changes from your competitors and seeing how services and products could be delivered differently. Often, it involves taking ideas from one sector to another.

Action

This is being keen to not only discover ideas and solution, but committing to taking action on them. Yet, it means also understanding that some ideas will fail and that you need to bounce back and try again. Action in enterprise is about trying, continuous improvement, and learning as you go.

Mind-set

The key element of having an enterprise mind-set is that you remain committed to taking something and improving it when others would have walked away. The desire to drive things forward enables you to overcome obstacles and put in the hard work required. This requires you to be "stretchy" in your thinking. A stretchy mind-set means stretching yourself outside your comfort zone and beyond in order to take on a new way of working and thinking to achieve your aims.

The power of the enterprise mind-set

Having an enterprise mind-set can often be the difference between the success and failure of a project. As the leader or manager, your role here is to support and encourage the development of an enterprise mind-set.

To have an enterprise mind-set, a person who possesses the attitudes and traits already considered then adds:

1) The ability to see the possibilities in a situation rather than the difficulties.

2) The ability to accept failure, and the will to try again having learnt from it.

3) The ability to see things from other people's view and provide solutions suitable for other people's needs.

Having an enterprise mind-set can really set an individual apart from others. It enables individuals to not only see a need, but to give things a try. This is coupled with the ability to bounce back when things don't go to plan. As long as their future decisions are influenced by lessons learnt, and mistakes are not repeated, then they are moving forward, improving, and increasing the likelihood of success.

In general, all of us could do with this mind-set to move through everyday challenges. It is worth considering that if more people had an enterprise mind-set, it could improve society as a whole. People with an enterprise mind-set focus on effort and action rather than lack of ability. They believe it is about trying and learning, not natural ability, skill, or intelligence. They want to improve things so that everyone benefits, customers, community, and the organisation they work for.

Staff who do not have this enterprise mind-set will say they can't and are unwilling to even try, often suggesting that it's not in their job role. I call these "Enterprise Blockers". However, don't presume that these staff members are purely negative. Often, these staff feel that their skills, abilities, and intelligence is fixed. They think no matter how hard they try, they cannot improve on what they have and are unlikely to succeed. They worry that they won't have the ability, and that even if they try, they will fail. It is possible that these staff are struggling to see how they can do something without losing face in front of others, or risking their job or future opportunities. Such staff members often waste energy and time lamenting on what should, could, or did happen rather than moving on and concentrating on the next step.

Staff with a more enterprising mind-set will focus on doing their best, accepting that if it doesn't work, they have at least tried. They have a "can do" attitude. They will often ask questions like "How can I…?" and "Why does that…?" They don't feel restricted to stay within set parameters. Furthermore, they don't feel that they are there to just achieve their present goals or work role, but to go beyond these targets, to achieve more.

On the whole, being enterprising is just about being willing to give something a try. As Amelia Earhart once said, "The most effective way to do it, is to do it". Being enterprising is similarly about *just doing it*. It is about having the right attitude and mind-set.

How much stretchiness do we need to have an enterprise mind-set?

When you take on any new way of doing things, you can either do so reluctantly, believing it is likely to fail and that you don't have the skills, experience, or ability. Or you can accept that it will require you to stretch yourself in a way you may never have done before.

Often, in order to develop an enterprising mind-set, you will need to stretch yourself to think about things in a different way and carry out activities in a different way. If you are asking staff to consider being enterprising for the first time, then you need to be aware that for some this is only a small stretch. However, others may feel stretched so far out of their comfort zone that they become uncomfortable and wish to return to where they feel at ease. It may take some people a lot of support and encouragement to achieve this new way of thinking and working.

Think of it just like an elastic band. Some elastic bands stretch really easily but can easily break or need to be used in conjunction with other elastic bands. Others are harder to stretch, but once stretched can be really strong and able to do a great job. Just like elastic bands, some staff will stretch easily and others not so easily, some will be great at stretching themselves while others are not so, and some will need to be stretched as part of a team.

Your role as the leader is to understand that everyone is different and some people are more willing to stretch than others, some will find it easier than others, and when staff seem difficult or resistant to change, it may just be that they not have seen the benefits in stretching yet.

Are specific age groups or type of employees more likely to be enterprising?

On the whole, you need to have a mixed group of people involved in any enterprise projects. This enables them each to bring their own experiences and ideas, but also their own way of thinking. Having a diverse range of ages, genders, and view points is invaluable.

However, it seems that generational expectations and views can impact on individuals' willingness to be involved and their ability to take part in more enterprising projects. For example, enterprise skills seem more evident within Generation X (those born approximately between 1965 and 1980), whilst Millennial or Generation Y (approximately 1981 – 2000) seem to find it easier to bring those enterprising traits to the fore.

Having a diverse range of staff will add value to any project and by mixing these staff together, they will become more aware of each others' views. These experiences can then be transferred into other areas of the business. Never underestimate how skills and knowledge can be transferred across the generations—both up and down.

We don't want mavericks in our organisation, thank you very much!

This is a common perception. Some employers worry that if they let someone take on a more enterprising role, the person will suddenly become a maverick. However, it's very unlikely that your staff will suddenly change completely. Though if they are currently a rule-breaker and you offer them the opportunity to be more enterprising and come up with new things, it's possible that the rule-breaking will not only continue, but increase. As always in leadership, it's down to you to manage these rule-breaking employees.

Generally, people who take on a more enterprising role within an organisation do so knowing that they are being trusted to do what's best for their employer. They are more likely to be cautious and considered in their decision-making. They will work with others in the organisation to ensure that the ideas are suitable and correctly implemented. It's your role as the manager to clarify the parameters within which their enterprise activities can take place.

How can I use enterprise in my organisation?

Senior management dictating initiatives to improve the organisation is what usually happens in organisations, both large and small. This book is about individuals being proactive in developing ideas throughout the organisation. This is a bottom-up, proactive way of working and is based around employee-led initiatives.

This system enables staff to take responsibility for activities that create a new approach within an organisation. This is contra to when one person, usually the most senior person within a large organisation, takes personal responsibility for taking an idea and ensuring it is followed through.

All enterprising activities should be rolled out with the fundamental potential of adding to the organisation's bottom line — increased income or profitability through innovative approaches. Such activities can be led by a collaborative group or an individual at any level within the organisation. These activities are pre-agreed and carried out within set parameters to reduce risk and increase success rates.

> **Consider this...**
>
> Big reality check! Just because you bought this book and know you need to change doesn't mean that your competitors aren't doing the same or may even be further ahead than you in the process of encouraging enterprise in their organisation. They too could be looking at ways to make their business different to help with the recruitment and retention of staff or to stay competitive.
>
>
>
> It's likely that they also know they need to grow, increase their customer loyalty, do more with less, and look at new ways of bringing in income and building a sustainable organisation. How likely are they to accept that staff need to be given more opportunity to be enterprising? So just think, if you are worried about losing control, you could be missing out while your competitors speed forward!

So why should you care about enterprise?

There are many reasons why you should consider encouraging enterprise within your organisation and these include:

Restless younger workforce

There is a swathe of younger workers who are restless. They have a desire to make a real impact in the world with their lives and careers. Many are turning to start-up companies for opportunities, while others are starting their own businesses. But there are also those who see that larger companies can make a bigger impact due to their size and resources.

These people see that they can be involved in great things by working within larger companies who allow them to do what they love. They also realise they will have access to the support and infrastructure of the organisation to do this.

However, if you don't enable these staff to be enterprising and get involved, they will leave or move to a more enterprising employer.

Staff retention

We know that staff retention can be a problem for organisations. Some companies find that they are losing their best and most talented staff members to their competitors. Staff members who don't feel their skills are being utilised to the full become frustrated and may seek an employer who is willing to offer them the opportunities to use these skills, develop new skills, and have new experiences. By offering staff opportunities to be enterprising, you can retain staff that may have been considering moving on.

Recruitment of high-quality staff members

Higher-level employees will only move to a new employer if they believe the move will offer them new opportunities and a longer-term development opportunity. By offering opportunities around enterprise development — and making sure people know you offer these opportunities — you'll find that recruiting and retaining high-flying staff becomes much easier.

Hold on: shouldn't the business development team be doing this?

You could be right there — this is probably one of the tasks your business development team do day in, day out. But this is about taking it a step further and encouraging *all* of your staff at every level and in every department to be seeking opportunities for your organisation to improve and develop.

Business development can be everyone's job, and by giving people the opportunity to take part in the growth of the organisation, it can take business development to a whole other level. However, if you do have a business development team, it's important for them to play a role in supporting staff and developing a more enterprising solution, so they do not feel their jobs are being eroded. Their roles can become more about facilitating ideas, rather than just working alone on developing ideas and rolling them out.

When done well, enterprise throughout an organisation will benefit your business development teams. This is because the rest of the organisation will be acting in a supportive way, rather than (possibly without realising it) hindering the business development team with negative actions and activities, those "Enterprise Blockers" I mentioned before.

> ### Case study
>
> In an educational organisation, the business development team were struggling to get local employers to buy the new solutions available. Through discussion, they discovered that the employers had poor experiences of working with the organisation previously, particularly some of the teaching staff who needed placements for their students. Even worse, they were continuing to find it difficult to work with the organisation as many staff members didn't value the relationship with the employers.
>
> By helping everyone in the organisation to understand

the importance of enterprise, this could have been changed and the staff could have adopted a more enterprising mind-set. For example, the teaching staff would begin to understand the importance of building up relationships with the employers. This would mean understanding their needs and how to add value as an educational establishment. All the staff could help by raising awareness of the organisation's offerings through outreach programs. By raising the profile, it assists the business development team when they need to connect outside the organisation.

What can you achieve through enterprise in your organisation?

Enterprise enables you to:

- Improve what you already do.
- Save money, reduce costs, and improve profits.
- Enter new markets with your current products.
- Develop new products or services.
- Enter new markets with new products.
- Set up a new business within the structure of your current operations—an internal start-up.
- Set up a new business alongside your current one but as a standalone option.
- Develop collaborative projects inside and outside your organisation's current work.

- Have a learning culture that encourages a stream of idea generation and pilot projects.

When you have identified an enterprise mind-set in your staff and have encouraged them to embrace it and make use of it, this will benefit the organisation. But how realistic is it to just ask someone, "Can you now add *being enterprising* to your job description please?" So let's take a deeper look at what we are expecting them to do.

What do enterprising staff do?

Enterprising staff are just your normal everyday team members doing their normal activities and duties. The divergence comes when they see a need for a different approach, a problem that can and should be fixed, or an opportunity that should be explored.

Having an enterprise mind-set is about recognising the integration and interdependency of each element of the business. It is about having the ability to see and the willingness to take action when something isn't working in the best interests of the customer or the company (preferably both at the same time).

Enterprising staff carry out tasks that are:

- non-routine
- somewhat complicated
- goal-orientated
- demanding but potentially achievable
- tackled in an adventurous manner
- approached in a determined and dynamic way
- help to accomplish or nearly accomplish the organisational goals

- things that require considerable effort to find an alternative solution.

Activities other than these are more likely to be normal work-based activities that do not require the staff member to be particularly enterprising.

> **Consider this...**
>
> Be careful you don't get sucked into the misconception that just by being innovative or creative, you are being enterprising. In fact, enterprising solutions do not have to be innovative, nor necessarily creative — just good ideas for your organisation and customers.
>
> Any change — be it creative, innovative, or just a simple idea brought in from elsewhere — should only be implemented if it will help achieve the organisation's aims. Those aims could be about increased customer satisfaction, commercial gain, or profit, or fulfilling obligations such as contracts and public duty in the case of public bodies.
>
> Be wary that it can be easy to do something innovative and believe it's a great idea without fully evaluating whether it will have a beneficial impact on the organisation.

Is enterprise about customers or people who use your services?

Bottom line, yes. Understanding clients' needs, wants, and expectations so that a business retains its customers is at the heart of enterprise. This is made possible by developing solutions to customer needs. But that doesn't mean blindly doing everything that customers want. The success of enterprise is about decision-making—being able to think critically and clearly, and develop solutions that suit the need of the client and fit the organisation's longer-term plans.

Developing enterprise projects is about placing the customer at the very heart of the business plans and enabling staff to provide what customers want and need in a timely manner.

Having an analytical way of thinking can really help in the decision-making process, however, it is also important to be customer-focused and curious. By encouraging your staff to be curious, they will question things and listen in order to find out information that will help develop the business.

Summary

- Enterprise is about using ideas to grow your organisation.
- Enterprising people come up with ideas and turn them into reality.
- Staff can develop ideas and solutions to problems, which can help the organisation's bottom line.
- Enterprise can really help with staff engagement and recruitment issues.
- Enterprising projects are those that are out of the ordinary.

PART TWO:

What Is the Enterprise Within™ System?

Chapter 2 –

Enterprise Within: the Process

"Even innovative and creative ideas need structure sometimes."

To develop longer-term benefits for your organisation, you should be considering implementing an integrated system into your organisation. This will enable staff members to actively participate in enterprise without the need to constantly ask for permission. It is often best to keep things as simple as possible, but you also need to accept that within larger organisations, you will need a system or a planned approach to ensure things run smoothly.

This chapter will cover:

- How the Enterprise Within™ system works on a practical level
- Taking you through the enterprise process step by step
- An overview of the process of developing an enterprising organisation

The basis of the system - the learning cycle

The Enterprise Within™ system is based on a core principle of the learning cycle of adults. Its overall aim is to enable team members and leaders to become more involved in a continuous development process. This is done by encouraging reflection, and developing the organisation through a continuous learning process. This is often referred to in education as the learning cycle based on the work of Kolb.

In his work on learning styles, Kolb developed his experiential learning cycle. He believed "Learning is the process whereby knowledge is created through the transformation of experience", or in other words, learning by giving things a go. This learning style is typically shown as the four stages that a learner goes through in order to progress in any area of personal growth. They are:

- **Concrete Experience** – Doing or having an experience, which may be a new experience or one encountered in a different way or in light of new knowledge or experiences.

- **Reflective Observation** – Reviewing and reflecting on the experience: what went well, what didn't go well, etc.

- **Abstract Conceptualization** – Considering what needs to change in order to improve the situation / experience: how you can modify or improve.

- **Active Experimentation** – Planning and trying the new idea or the improved idea based on what you learnt / observed.

As this is a cycle of continuous improvement, the learner then returns to step one—they actually try it, reflect, and then retry. This process serves individuals well when developing a more enterprising way of working, due to the need to try, test, review, and alter an idea in order to find the best solution possible.

The Enterprise Within™ system

The Enterprise Within™ system is based on the learning

cycle process to ensure that changes are carefully considered, tested, and reviewed on a continuous basis. Some additional steps have been included to ensure that the individual is certain the idea is possible with the teams and skills available to them. The simple enterprise process is shown here:

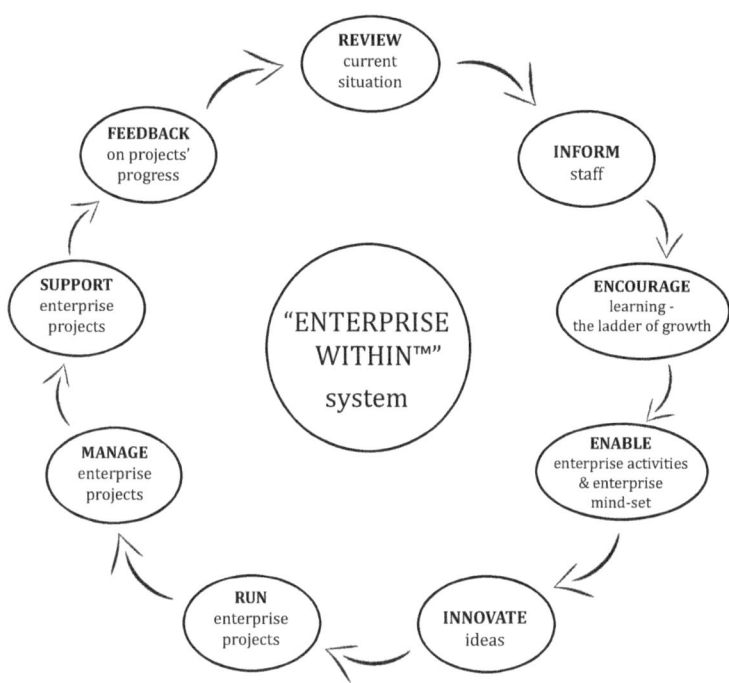

REVIEW current situation

As with any organisational change, you need to start at the beginning and look at the current situation. Consider the following questions:

- Where does your income come from?

- Which areas of the organisation could be improved?
- What ideas / projects could be replicated in other areas of the organisation?
- How is the organisation doing in relation to its competitors?
- What does your marketplace look like, what changes are you expecting, and are you ready for them?
- Does the organisation have a clear vision for the future?
- Is there a development plan, business plan, etc? Does it need updating?

Of course, you may think of many more questions as you work through this element of the process. Your aim is to review the current situation and consider how it fits into the work of developing a more enterprising and sustainable organisation.

One of the fundamental areas of enterprise is the ability to adapt your services or products to meet the needs of your customers. This is about developing a way of maintaining and growing your business to ensure its future. It means knowing what customers need and whether you are offering the right solutions. This is not about knee-jerk reactions and always providing what customers want without question. Rather, it is about listening to what they need and considering whether and how you can offer these options. In addition, you need to have an eye on the future. What will people need, how will they want to access services and receive products, etc?

All ideas and solutions must, of course, be of added value to the organisation. It's easy to be busy "being enterprising". However, if the activity is not helping with the bottom line (be it making profits, or if you are a funded or not-for-profit organisation, providing quality resources), then it is a distraction. It is not helping you in the longer term.

Consider what the organisation needs to be more stable and sustainable

To be more stable and sustainable for the future, you as a leader need to be thinking of what the organisation currently does in order to consider what it can add or improve on.

When developing a more enterprising way of working, you need to consider the following three main areas of enterprise:

a. Ways you can save money for the organisation by adopting a more enterprising approach.

b. Ways you can increase profits / revenue by doing what you already do but in a different way, an improved way, or to a new client group.

c. Things you can do in addition to your current offerings that could bring in new income streams.

Enterprise Options

Each of these three ways can improve the organisation's profitability and stability, but it's unlikely that you could consider all three straight away. You need to consider what is most needed for your current situation. For example, if the organisation is in a vulnerable position with poor cash flow, it might be more important to focus on reducing costs through improving stock management. You can then move on to increasing short-term income by coming up with promotional activities. Finally, you can start looking at new markets or new ideas to move your work forward. On the other hand, if the organisation has a strong financial position but is missing out on opportunities due to a lack of options for customers, it may be time to consider developing a new element of your work.

The reality of enterprise solutions is that you need to develop agility in your teams. Enterprise agility is about having a more responsive way of working, adapting to changes in need, and adapting to the environment you work in. All of this whilst knowing and being aware of what you are trying to achieve and what needs to be altered in order to move forward. It is, therefore, very important that you fully understand where you are right now.

INFORM staff

It's really common for leaders to skip this element of enterprise development, often believing that their staff members already know what the plans are for the organisation, or feeling that their staff don't need to know. However, in reality, staff don't always know key information about the organisation's current and planned situations. They need to understand why you want to embrace enterprise, so you need to provide a compelling reason why they should get involved.

When staff don't feel informed or don't understand why the change is needed, they can become unconnected and uninvolved. This leads to them being unwilling to get involved in your enterprise projects, due to a lack of understanding of the implications and benefits to them.

> **Consider this…**
>
> Do your staff understand the plans for the future, the vision of the organisation? If not, how best can you inform them and keep them involved? Maybe you could bring all of the staff together for an update, a Q&A with the leaders, or share it in smaller groups, team meetings, or through technology-based communication options.

Make sure the messages are consistent. If you are unable to give everyone the same message at the same time, make sure the information is clear and can't be misconstrued. You may be saying "We need to be enterprising in order to grow and become even better than we are". But staff who feel excluded or vulnerable may be hearing a different message. Something like "The business needs to change, things aren't good, we need to be enterprising to survive, and if you're not enterprising, you're at risk."

In addition, if staff are not informed about what direction you wish the organisation to move in, they may offer unsuitable suggestions. Without this key information, they are unlikely to come up with ideas for the future of the organisation that suit the overall plans.

To ensure that staff members feel involved and able to contribute to the business, they need to not only understand the vision of the organisation, but also how the company is aiming to reach that vision. This will enable staff to spot suitable opportunities that are in line with the company's plans.

Leaders need to ensure more honest communication about the organisation as a whole. This means honesty about how it runs, what is key to its future, and what is important to its board and senior executives. It is impossible for staff to know what they can do to help the organisation if they are unaware of how it runs, what it needs, and where it's going. Staff need at least a basic business understanding.

> ### Case study
>
> A CEO once told me that a staff member came to them with an idea of how they could move the organisation forward. It was a relatively simple idea that would see them move into providing products in a different marketplace. It only required some very simple modifications to their existing product. The staff member couldn't believe how easy it would be and was surprised that no one had spotted the opportunity sooner.
>
>
>
> But the CEO dismissed the idea. "How stupid," he said to me, "Doesn't he know that we are planning to drop that product as it is no longer profitable?" But how would the staff member know that the product wasn't profitable or that the board were planning to drop it unless they had been informed? It wasn't a stupid idea — just one that didn't fit the longer-term plans of the organisation.

Staff members may find it hard to develop an idea if they are unaware of business activities and lack knowledge on how to run a business, particularly in areas such as profit and loss, marketing, product placement, etc. Often, they do not know what the organisation is focusing on or planning for the future. This then leads to frustration when they develop an idea and it is thrown out as being not suitable because of plans they were unaware of.

ENCOURAGE learning – the ladder of growth

When developing an enterprising organisation, learning becomes a core element of the development. Enterprise is about developing a learning organisation. A learning organisation encourages individuals and teams to support each other, learn from each other, and grow together. This means asking your team to be stretchy, not just flexible. Flexibility is about slightly altering things, but we are asking staff to really stretch themselves and take on new skills and new ways of thinking, and this requires them to be stretchy. Your role as the leader is to help them be more stretchy and provide opportunities for them to grow and develop.

You can use this book to take stock of your ability as an organisation from a resources and ability point of view. You need to know how able your teams are. Are they lacking in any skills, knowledge, or abilities? Consider what learning needs to be encouraged so that staff feel equipped and able to develop ideas and move forward. Many organisations already carry out staff skills audits and this can be amended to include a review of enterprise skills and an enterprise mind-set.

The overall theory is to become a collaborative, agile team that shares knowledge and is actively involved in personal and team learning — rather than having competitive individuals out for their own gain. The individual steps to develop a learning organisation that enables enterprise to take place can be found here:

Embrace a Learning Organisation

Show staff how learning is a complete organisational development tool, not just something for an individual.

Support Learning

Provide ways for staff to learn. Encourage them to not only learn but use what they have learnt.

Encourage Knowledge Transfer

Knowledge is more beneficial to an organisation when shared. Encourage structured sharing of knowledge.

Develop Resilience

Resilient people accept that failure is part of life and can bounce back. Help staff learn how to do this.

Action Learning

Enable staff to learn through activities. Provide them with a way to try, review, and reflect so they can progress and improve.

Enable Proactive Staff

Provide staff with the structure and levels of empowerment needed to be more proactive in their approach.

Fuel Curiosity

Help staff to develop a curious mind so they look out for ideas and opportunities they can bring back to your organisation.

Innovation and Idea Generation

Enterprise Within™

ENABLE enterprise activities

It is your role as a leader to ensure that enterprising activities are allowed to happen. This can be as simple as informing staff that they can do things or come up with ideas and present them to you – or implementing a full organisational approach to enable staff to be more enterprising, as laid out in this book.

Consider how you can implement a simple approach

If you are new to enterprise within your organisation, it's best to consider a simple approach first. Try running activities during staff meetings where people can raise ideas and work them through with their team. Provide simple forms where they can develop the ideas and put them forward. Then, offer a system of decision-making so that staff understand how their idea is considered for future development. In addition, be clear what involvement staff will have and what support they will be offered if their idea is actually taken up.

Provide a structured decision-making process

It is important to avoid staff members becoming frustrated with their employers because project ideas are not being taken up or are slow to progress. If an organisation's decision-making process is unclear or not explained, staff can feel their ideas are falling into a black hole, never to be seen again. This can be because there were too many people involved in the decision-making process or because there was no clear process. It can even be that the ideas were not suitable but no one gave the staff feedback on them.

You need to make it clear how ideas should be put forward, who will look at them, and how the decision-maker will decide which ideas are considered. You need to explain how the process works, offer feedback on unsuccessful ideas, and provide a system of support for people whose ideas have been accepted.

> **Consider this...**
>
> Provide a simple form that can be completed by a staff member and submitted to the senior team, potentially via their manager. In the form, ask for an explanation of their idea, how they see it working, and how they would like to be involved, or whether they wouldn't like to be involved. Make it clear who will review their idea and how they will receive feedback on it.
>
> Keep your system simple and clear for staff so they know their ideas are worth putting forward.

Enable staff to be responsive but strategic

Much of the smaller-scale enterprise agility is about being responsive to need and customer requirements. The crucial element here is for staff to know the parameters in which they operate or what decisions they can and can't make.

> **Developing stretchy staff**
>
> Let's take a member of waiting staff in your hotel as an example. A client complains about the quality of the food. What level of decision-making does the staff member have over this? Can they decide to offer an alternative, discount the bill, or even waive the bill? What options do staff members have to avoid similar problems in the future?

Can they let the chef know that it is a recurring issue or bring it up at staff meetings? Should they only bring it up if they know why it's occurring? Maybe it's due to lack of clarity on the menu when people order, or possibly the quality of the ingredients being purchased? Should they only bring it up if they have a possible idea or solution?

Non-stretchy staff would say "Well it was just a complaint and these things happen." A stretchy staff member would want to know why it happened and what can be done to stop it happening again.

Staff need to know what decisions they can make to improve the quality of the business and customer experience both instantly and in the longer term. Do they have a level of discretionary spending or level of authority before they need to seek more support for their idea or possible actions?

They need to understand that responsiveness is good, but it must be considered so it doesn't have a negative impact on the organisation.

Developing larger scale enterprise projects

If you're planning on running larger scale enterprise projects, let staff know how they can get involved if they want to be. In addition, you may want to encourage other staff members to put themselves forward as support, especially if they have a skill or are knowledgeable in a particular area that may be beneficial to develop an enterprising project.

When developing larger scale projects, keep an eye on bureaucracy, as it is one of the main reasons why enterprising ideas are not implemented, or why staff don't bother to even put forward their idea. The aim here is to have enterprising projects that enable the organisation to be more fluid. Ideas often need to be evolving and developing in a responsive way.

INNOVATE ideas

For many organisations, coming up with an idea is easy. In fact, they have too many ideas and their main task is to identify the right one. For others, they wonder how they can develop innovative ideas. If you're trying to discover and come up with new ideas or have ideas but want to be sure they are the right ones, you should consider what type of ideas you need.

Consider what your customers need

Customers are becoming more demanding and more aware of what your competitors are offering. There has never been a more competitive time for any organisation. Even those who offer public services are finding people more demanding and more willing to complain, or seek other solutions. You need to develop solutions that are client-focused.

Consider what need there is for your idea. Whilst you might think it's great, do other people — your potential customers — even want what you're considering offering? It's easy to fall into the trap of believing there's a need for something because no one else is providing it, when it may be that no one else is providing it because there is no need for it.

Need is not about what you think is needed, but what genuinely is needed and will be utilised and paid for.

Case study

A community charity decided that because there was no cinema in their town, there would be a need. They believed they could offer a community service that would also bring in an income. Keen to move ahead, they identified a venue and even the equipment and how to access films. But no one had really looked into the need — was there enough need in the local area to justify opening a cinema? Once they had considered the need and the costs and success levels of other community cinemas, they changed their minds. But this could have become a costly mistake. The team were sure that there was a need because there was no local provision and because several of them felt they would love to go to the cinema more often, but the research proved otherwise.

Explore the options available to you

Enterprising projects that fail often do so because the first solution or idea has been implemented. Enterprise is often seen as something that will bring instant results. However, for quality longer-term results, it is necessary to consider all the options and take the time to decide on the best idea or solution.

Sometimes, when we start out considering enterprising solutions, we think of the simplest ideas or those closest to home, i.e. the most similar to what we already do. But sometimes you need to explore further afield, and even consider collaborating with others, or moving into a new area of work. I'm not talking about moving into something completely new necessarily, but something that complements what you already offer and the skills of your team.

Thinking bigger can be the key to success in enterprise. Keeping things small and safe can lead to poor results or a low return on the level of investment made. Take the time to evaluate all the options. Often, different opportunities can lead to similar results, so it's important to find the right option for your organisation.

RUN enterprise projects

This is about giving staff the opportunity to develop the skills, mind-set, and culture to create an engaged workforce. It is about providing them with a structured support program or system that they can follow. It needs to be simple but effective in encouraging staff to come forward with ideas and try their ideas out.

Encourage your staff members to take part in general learning and knowledge development around enterprise and business development. But don't rely on theory alone. It is also important to offer opportunities to learn by being involved in enterprise activities. Here are some activities to take their learning and turn it into action to encourage enterprise in your organisation.

Business case requests

Provide individuals with simple training or coaching support to develop their idea into a business case. This avoids poorly considered ideas being tried out or put forward. Using a template or pre-agreed format can ensure the idea is thoroughly considered before it is presented to a senior staff member for a decision. In addition, you can also implement a structured approach to consider and ideas and feed back on a business case.

Master classes

Bringing in individuals with expertise can be really valuable. Consider people who are able to help in areas such as developing an enterprise culture and the various elements of enterprise such as idea generation, developing an idea, and taking an idea to market. Give staff the business skills they need to know without overloading them. It's not necessary for them to know every element, but having an understanding can help ensure the success of an enterprise project.

Hackathon

Often used in tech companies as well as banks and universities, a hackathon is an event where staff members from various sections of an organisation are brought together, usually over a solid 24-hour period, to consider, develop, or come up with ideas for the organisation. Often led by an external facilitator or consultant, it brings together staff as well as internal and external experts who can work together to develop ideas. At the beginning of the day, an idea or various ideas are considered, teams of people work on the idea, and by the end of the 24 hours, see whether they have a viable idea to move forward with. Many events culminate in the teams presenting their ideas to the senior team of the organisation for consideration.

Innovation days

Innovation days are often facilitated by an external innovation consultant and are carried out by staff members brought together from various elements of the organisation. The innovation days are used to come up with a variety of ideas, which may or may not be viable to move forward with. These days are often used to start generating ideas and demonstrate to staff that it is possible for them to generate their own ideas.

More and more these days are also run with local schools and colleges to bring added value to the school, a better connection for the organisation, and opportunities for staff to connect with younger people. If you have never spent the day carrying out innovation workshops with a group of young people, then do it—as you can often be inspired by their naturally innovative approach.

Enterprise proposals (often run as a competition)

You can also ask staff to come up with ideas alone or in groups and put their idea forward using a structured project proposal form, potentially with a presentation by those submitting the idea. The form is often loosely based on a business plan format, and is then judged by a team of internal and external individuals. The staff whose ideas are selected can then be offered a fixed amount of time and/or money to develop the idea further.

Since agility is often the driver for encouraging enterprise, having a very simple process to encourage responsive and rapid enterprise activities in your organisation may be beneficial. Consider informing staff that you are interested in hearing their ideas and provide them with various ways to bring them forward and implement them.

Enterprise champions

This means having staff members who are trained in supporting, encouraging, and mentoring staff members who have an idea. Staff members can then directly approach these champions to develop their idea ready for consideration. Champions are often strategically placed within departments and are supported by the senior executive team, the learning and development team, and the business development team. They can also be involved with enterprise days and hackathons, and use their knowledge to support enterprise in the community, in schools, etc.

Mastermind groups or peer-to-peer learning

It can often be valuable to bring groups of people together from various departments within your organisation, or indeed people from other organisations, known as "mastermind groups". In these groups, there is usually a common element such as innovation, project management, or launching a new product. The group meets to discuss the members' projects and individuals help each other resolve problems or consider questions. Together, the group can work through issues using shared knowledge and experiences to develop their ideas. These groups are often run by a facilitator and are usually made up of individuals who don't work together.

Mentors

Mentors can be particularly powerful in assisting an individual gain confidence in their own skills and abilities as an enterprising person. Having a well-placed senior staff member as a mentor can support an individual in accessing the right support and information to move their project forward.

You will need to decide the best way to run enterprise projects in your organization, should they be large-scale multidisciplinary projects or smaller, discreet ones with minimal fuss and support. Indeed, they can be projects simply based on someone having an idea, developing a plan for implementing the idea, and providing some management support to ensure the idea is implemented and is successful.

MANAGE enterprise projects

As the leader or manager, your role is to enable the enterprising staff member to carry out their work. You need to provide them with the right tools at the right time and ensure their skills are being developed along the way to enable the project to be as successful as possible.

Ensure the organisation has the tools and structure to move forward

The easiest way to encourage staff to have an enterprising mind-set is to support a learning organisation model of sharing knowledge and problem-solving in teams. Use staff meetings to discuss options and opportunities, and work through ideas and possibilities in a positive way to enable everyone to learn and grow.

Consider what other tools and formats you can utilise that would suit your organisation in order to encourage staff to develop an enterprising mind-set and encourage knowledge sharing or continuous learning.

SUPPORT enterprise projects

This means encouraging and supporting staff to come up with solutions and work through them without the constant need for senior leaders to be involved. This enables your organisation to respond flexibly.

If you have staff who fail to work on their own initiative, then examine the situation to see whether this is because they are concerned with compliance, procedures, use of time, or achieving the targets set by managers. Understand that embedding enterprise is a continual development process, so you need to find a way to support your staff members in accepting this new enterprising way of working.

Doing so requires two-way feedback, which means you need to listen to your team members even if what they are saying can be hard to hear. Your role here as the leader is to enable enterprise to happen, so if their feedback is that they are having difficulties, facing barriers, or experiencing resistance from other departments, then you need to help them overcome these issues. You can only do this by involving yourself in feedback conversations.

Learn from experience

You can enable staff to learn from experience using a range of options, such as:

- Mentoring and coaching.
- Mastermind / learning circles.
- Reflective learning.
- Self-directed learning.

If you are looking to develop a more enterprising organisation or department, you need to accept that there is going to be an element of cultural change involved. Be aware that staff can feel overwhelmed if they are involved in lots of initiatives, so try to keep your enterprise projects as simple as possible. Ask staff what they feel they can take on, listen to their needs, and ask them to consider what support they require.

Anyone in an organisation can be enterprising. So support the staff at all levels to explore enterprise — you may be surprised who has the desire and ability to be enterprising.

FEED BACK on enterprise projects

If you as a leader have decided to invest in being more enterprising, then you need to invest some of your time in giving feedback. Ensure you feed back to managers and staff members about the progress they are making, the ideas they are coming up with, and the results they are achieving. Feedback is key to building staff confidence and encouraging them to develop even more ideas in the future. Think of yourself as an "Enterprise Enabler": a person who encourages and makes enterprise happen by working with and supporting their team.

Finally, you should be continuously reviewing how you embed enterprise within your organisation. Enterprise is a tool for continuous improvement, not a one-off solution and quick fix. Often, an organisation starts with small enterprise projects and ideas, but by continuously carrying out the Enterprise Within™ system, they can develop those ideas into larger projects with greater levels of impact.

Summary

To develop a more enterprising way of working in your organisation, you will need to:

- Review where you are as an organisation.
- Review how to move forward by considering organisational need, customer need, and the options open to you.
- Give staff a structured process so they can be empowered to make decisions.
- Provide a way of enabling continuous improvement and learning.

PART THREE:

How to Embed Enterprise Within™ *in Your Organisation*

Find the best path for your organisation, customers, and employees

Chapter 3 –

Enterprise Needs Structure to Be Flexible

"Structure needn't quash enterprise – it can enable it to thrive if agile, considered, and prudent."

In order to stay competitive, organisations need to be more agile in how they respond to change. By embracing enterprise, your organisation can alter the way it works, grows, and outmanoeuvres its competitors. This requires the ability to be adaptable and the knowledge of how to deal with predicted change, as well as the unpredicted. By having a structured approach to enterprise, you can reap the rewards.

This chapter will cover:

- The benefits of enterprise
- The structure needed to enable enterprise
- How to encourage enterprise agility for your organisation
- The key ingredients needed for an organisation to be enterprising

Running an organisation is more than just developing products or services for sale. It's about considering how teams work together to help the organisation grow and respond to changes in the market. Reacting to these changes in a positive and strategic way is vital to the long-term stability of any organisation.

The more enterprise agility you and your teams have, the easier it is to deal with whatever changes come your way. You will feel more comfortable adapting and changing when faced with complex problems, crises, and fierce competition if you have a more agile way of working and responding. As you have grown and learnt to develop together, you and your team will find it easier to adapt as you will know your strengths and weaknesses, both as an organisation and as a team.

What's needed to enable more enterprise within your organisation

In order to develop an agile, enterprising way of working within your organisation, it is important to consider the processes and structure of the business. An organisation must consider the following elements and how they link together:

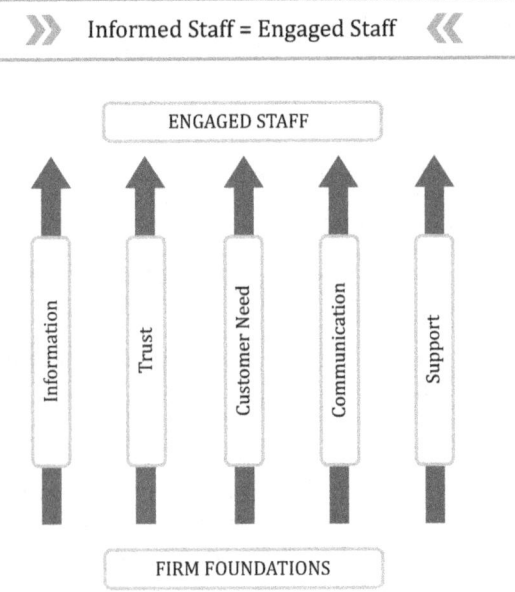

Firm foundations: to prevent your enterprise from crumbling

A solid business with focus and strategy will always find it easier to embrace an enterprising culture. To ensure the foundation you are building on is solid, consider the following:

1) Do your staff at all levels know the core reasons why your organisation exists? Is there a reason why this organisation functions and if so, do they know why and how important it is to stay to true to those core reasons?

2) Does your organisation have an overall plan or strategy for the future? Do your staff know what this plan is?

3) Does your organisation have a vision statement that all the employees buy into, and do your staff know, understand, and follow it?

The clearer and more solid the foundations, the easier it is for your teams to develop enterprising ideas that will be beneficial to your organisation's long-term plans. For example, if your hotel business wishes to focus less on the holiday travel market and more on the business market, your team need to know this so any ideas they develop to move the business forward are focused on business travellers.

Consider this...

For those of you working in public bodies and charities, this is where you need to be aware of and consider your ethos and core purpose. What is the fundamental reason that your organisation exists and do your enterprising ideas add to your core operations or distract from it?

Information: to provide valuable staff members with clarity

To avoid poor decision-making, staff need up-to-date and clear information so they understand the needs and possibilities. When informed, they are able to understand the whole situation rather than having their views clouded by incomplete or unconnected ideas. When staff are trying to develop enterprising solutions without knowledge of the bigger picture, it can be at best frustrating and at worst costly and harmful to the long-term sustainability of the organisation.

Case study

One such company I worked with felt it wasn't important to explain to staff how critical the organisation's financial situation was. The business was within weeks of closing its doors, yet managers asked staff to develop some enterprising solutions to bring in much-needed additional revenue.

The staff members started investing time and effort into looking for new income streams, but whilst they did that, they took their eye off the day-to-day work. Soon, the company was spiralling out of control as the staff became distracted with possible ideas and stopped focusing on what was bringing in the money now. It needed drastic action and that action was honesty. The staff needed to hear the reality from the senior team. Once they could see how bad things really had become, they could see that their efforts needed to be put into bringing in money today and not considering what could bring them in income in the future.

Information or lack of it affected the team's understanding of the full situation. This led to them looking for the wrong type of enterprising solution. The more that staff have knowledge of the real situation, the easier it is for them to make decisions that help the business right now. Whilst it was a struggle, they are still trading many years later. Some staff chose to move on, not willing to remain in an organisation that was precarious. But others were willing to face the future in the full knowledge of how things were and what needed to be done. They took up the challenge and helped the organisation survive.

Trust: A two-way process

To enable your staff to be more enterprising, they need

some freedom to develop, consider ideas, work on solutions, and experiment with options. This requires trust. You need to trust them that they are getting on with things in an acceptable way. You have to trust that they will not jeopardise the organisation through poor decisions or unconsidered actions. For enterprise to come from the bottom up rather than enforced from the top down, you need to decrease your involvement or you will have too much influence on the ideas.

However, trust works both ways. Your teams need to trust you too. They must trust that you have their back—that you are there to support, encourage, and enable them to do their work. When staff members are unsure of the consequences or the level of support from their senior team, their decisions will be less bold, and their actions conservative. This is not beneficial.

If there is just one thing that you take from this book, then this is it: no staff member will put themselves or their job on the line to take action unless they trust that:

- Someone has their back.
- Everyone understands that they are doing it for the right reasons.
- They are in full receipt of the information needed to move their idea forward.
- Others are there to help and support, not to hinder or sabotage.

Customer need: always a core element to enterprise

Placing the customer at the core of business decisions is vital. Let's be realistic here, you can develop all sorts of ideas, but if your customers or potential customers don't like the offering or the way it is offered, there is little chance of your enterprise project being successful.

When staff are considering new ideas and being more enterprising, the customer must be considered throughout the process. Help staff by asking them key questions such as:

1) Is this something our customers want or need?

2) Is this being offered in a way that our customers would be willing to pay for?

3) Are our services being provided in a way people can easily use?

4) How realistic is it for us to get our current or future customers to buy into this idea?

Too many enterprising ideas fail because they have not been considered from the customer's point of view. Don't forget that the customers' needs can change and you will need to keep changing with them. For example, remember the movie rental shops we used to see on our high street? When online streaming of movies began, these businesses failed. They were already struggling and a new kid on the block caused their final demise. They didn't believe or see a time coming when people would no longer wish to hire DVDs and videos, even though it would mean avoiding late return fees and the hassle of going to the store. Being aware of changing needs is vital in selecting the way forward for your organisation.

Developing stretchy staff

Whilst we put customers at the core of our decisions, don't fall into the trap of believing you understand customers' needs from a handful of throwaway comments. Just because some of your faithful clients say they would buy something doesn't mean it's worth developing the idea without further research.

A stretchy staff member would consider any new enterprise project carefully and see things from different perspectives, learn about the marketplace, and carry out some quality market research before taking it forward.

Communication: to keep everyone on the same page and heading in the same direction

This is nothing new, is it? Communication (or lack of it) regularly causes projects to fail. This is either because information is unknown or people are unaware of the plan of action. When staff have not been communicated to in the right way about enterprise within an organisation, it can cause difficulties. This can lead to staff feeling confused and vulnerable, and left searching for answers.

It's important to continuously communicate to people, both inside and outside the organisation, who are working on the enterprise project's aims, plan, and progress. This ensures that everyone involved can identify whether they have anything valuable to add, and ensure they understand why the project is being carried out.

Case study

Work on a major project for one of my clients was moving ahead at a great pace. The idea was to develop a new way of delivering print services to clients. The new digital solution provided a faster response to customer needs. The team behind it were thrilled with the progress — digital printing of products that could be printed, finished, and delivered overnight. Only days ahead of its launch, they presented the new offering to other staff members in the company.

But there was a problem. No one had been aware of this new plan and the procurement team had altered the delivery firms they were using in order to reduce costs, so they no longer had pickups after 4pm. This meant that to have a printed product to a client by the next day, they would need to have received the files, printed them, carried out any finishing work (trimming, folding, etc.), and packaged it ready to leave by 4pm. What was worse, they had only just agreed to the new terms from the delivery company days before.

The lack of communication about the plans led to a swift change in the delivery company as well as having to promote a longer turnaround rather than the same day offering they had planned. Not really what the team had planned for, nor as competitive in a difficult marketplace.

Support: it needs to be more than "I'm here if you need me"

When staff are asked to go off and develop new ideas, work on their own initiative, and develop new solutions, management must consider the need for support. Each individual will require different levels of support, depending on the project or their experience. So you need to know when and how to do that.

Support in an enterprising environment is about providing light-touch guidance and high levels of encouragement and motivation. Support needs to be more about mentoring than providing solutions. When staff members are working on enterprising ideas, elements can go wrong, and ideas need to be reworked and taken right back to the drawing board. Many staff members worry that they are being judged — that others are seeing their efforts as failures, not a step closer to finding the right solution. It is at this time that a supportive leader can make all the difference. The leader has the enterprising individual's back and understands that progress may appear slow to others.

Engaged staff: a must for enterprising environments

In order to encourage your staff to be more enterprising, they need to be engaged in the organisation first. And the more involved in enterprising ideas they are, the more engaged they become. This may seem like a chicken and egg situation. However, you have to start somewhere and if your staff are disengaged, then starting with smaller enterprising projects that have quick results can lead to a dramatic increase in engagement. The importance of communication and sharing information can't be stressed enough here. Staff engagement and enterprising activities grow and increase over time. There needs to be a process that enables staff to submit ideas, and know how and when they will be reviewed and considered.

Engagement comes from a willingness and desire to be involved. If someone is asked to become involved in a project or an idea that they don't really want to do, they will either refuse or they will just contribute with a low level of enthusiasm. So you need to think what would encourage your staff to be involved in long-term development of the company.

Consider this…

Let's be honest here, none of this is rocket science. I am merely advocating that you allow your staff to speak up and be heard, join in with the development of your organisation, and take responsibility for building a sustainable plan for the future.

But what I do know is that this needs to be done in a structured way with parameters to keep an element of control and an organised way of doing things. This is about having multi-level communication in order to identify options for the future of the organisation. You need to provide your staff with a safe and suitable way of speaking up. In order to turn your customers' needs into new ideas that suit your organisation, you must have a good working grasp of your business and so must your team.

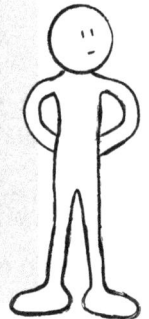

To build a more enterprising organisation, you will need to look at all of these elements: communication, trust, sharing information, providing support, and understanding customer need. Consider how all of this together can provide a more stable platform to develop enterprising ideas. When you have these elements, it can only serve to enhance the engagement of your staff and their willingness to become more enterprising.

Enterprise within an organisation is a composite way of working, as it needs a variety of elements to come together to enable the organisation to grow. At its heart, it supports staff so that they can enable the organisation to grow by listening, observing, and learning, and then sharing this knowledge with others for the benefit of the organisation.

Summary

Enterprise within an organisation requires the following elements:

- Firm foundations.
- Knowledge and a willingness for it to be shared freely.
- Trust—both up and down the chain of command as well as peer-to-peer.
- An understanding of customer needs and how this must be at the core of all decision-making.
- The unwavering support and encouragement of everyone within the organisation.
- An engaged workforce.

Chapter 4 –

Future-proof Your Organisation with Staff Engagement and Enterprise

"Engaged staff will support enterprising activities; disengaged staff will thwart them."

Employee engagement is the emotional commitment an employee has to the organisation and its goals. This affects the level of effort they put in. The more an employee is engaged, the more they put in the effort. This will result in a better service to customers and higher retention of staff, as well as increased productivity. By enabling higher levels of engagement, customer loyalty improves and profits increase.

Think of it like this. When you go into a shop and the staff are uninterested in you, or their company and its products, you will be less likely to buy, recommend, or return to the shop again. So how do you create a more engaged workforce, one where your employees are interested not just in the customers, but the long-term development of the organisation, and what would it look like?

This chapter will cover:

- What is staff engagement?
- What are the benefits of staff engagement?
- How do you improve staff engagement?
- Can you measure engagement?

What is needed to encourage staff engagement?

The core of staff engagement is creating an environment where staff elect to work to their full potential and put in their best efforts. This requires you to develop a relationship based on trust and commitment to one another. Show your employees you care about them. Consider whether your actions show that you appreciate your staff or not. It can be as simple as ensuring they have a nice place to work. How can you expect staff to feel valued if they are working in a scruffy office with a leaking roof? Show them you are committed to them. How can you expect staff to be committed if they have employment contracts that leave them feeling vulnerable with no prospects? How could you ask them for commitment if you show no commitment to them?

Employee engagement is about staff members each knowing their role within the organisation, i.e. what they bring to the table. Include them in the business process so they understand their importance to the success of the organisation. When staff are in control, aware of their role, and know what is expected of them, they feel valued and part of the bigger picture. Then, it becomes easier for them to see why they are important, and that by doing their very best and connecting to the organisation, they can influence its future prosperity. By allowing staff to take an element of control and feel connected, they feel pride in what they are working on or achieving.

For example, a member of staff working in a warehouse may not see how their work affects the overall performance and profit of the company. However, when they become involved in enterprising solutions as part of a team, they will start to understand the importance of their role in providing the customer with a good experience. Then they will feel that their role is of great value to the success of the organisation.

For staff to fully take advantage of being engaged, you need to encourage them to share. Those who are not listened to will soon become frustrated and will either leave or stop making any effort. They need to feel involved, and that means as a leader you will need to keep them informed whilst enabling them to input into the organisational plans.

> **Case study**
>
> When working with a community-based education provider, the team were excited to be able to help and quickly came up with some possible enterprise projects they could investigate. They presented their ideas to the senior team, who seemed pleased. But weeks went by with nothing happening. The staff started to question their ideas…maybe they were no good, maybe the senior team didn't think they were capable?
>
> After some time, the senior team announced an idea they had for an enterprise project. The ball was already rolling—it was happening, no discussions, no involvement, and not one of the ideas presented by the team. Yet the team were expected to buy into the idea and implement it. The trouble was they now felt uninvolved and when the project started to falter some months later, the team were not committed to its success and felt like it should never have gone ahead.
>
> Getting buy-in from staff is important, as is communicating why an idea can or can't occur. Staff need to feel empowered and involved in this process.

Trust and empowerment

You cannot get employee engagement through bribery,

promise of a better future, emotional manipulation, or scare tactics. There are no shortcuts to having a more engaged team. It requires two-way trust between you and your staff, and empowering your staff to take control and make decisions.

If you don't trust your staff members to carry out a requested action, then there is no point in talking about empowerment. Staff need to take responsibility for their actions or lack of actions. When they take responsibility and achieve something, they will begin to have an increasing feeling of pride in their work and feel more engaged in the business.

Empowerment and trust have to be built over time. Enterprise projects can enable this to happen by providing staff with opportunities to get involved and demonstrate their skills outside their usual role.

It's important to realise that just saying that you are empowering staff doesn't mean they will understand and value that. Many staff members fear taking a stand and doing something different. Taking a stand requires courage, as staff may fear trying something different and failing — and therefore looking bad in front of their colleagues. It's important that employees understand trying and failing is part of moving forward. They need to be confident that no one will laugh at the failure, but will offer encouragement and support to try again. This will help employees overcome the barrier of not wishing to try something new.

Staff need to take responsibility to achieve change

For many staff members, change is seen as something negative, something to fear. They see it as a way of checking up on them or catching them out, or questioning their ability. Their past experiences of change often cloud their judgment of future potential. So when they are empowered to make decisions for themselves, they often see this as something set to test them or trip them up. They fear it will be a way of spotting their weaknesses and therefore a way of dismissing them from their role.

However, staff members do need to take on a level of responsibility and accept that this is their role, for which they are recompensed. They need to be aware that they have the choice to either stay as they are, which may risk their role being placed under scrutiny, or they can become more involved and engaged in order to personally grow, and in return help the organisation grow. For many, whilst they fear the idea initially, once they begin to see how they are developing and moving along with the organisational changes, they can see the benefits for themselves and their long-term employability.

To help staff deal with change and develop a more empowered way of working, they must trust you as the leader. They have to trust that you will support them and encourage them even if they make a mistake. In order to do this, you need to encourage a culture of learning, demonstrating that when mistakes are made, the important thing is learning from them, rather than blaming someone.

Which people are right for you?

Attracting, developing, and retaining the right staff takes time and dedication. When you have the right people on board, you don't want them to leave because they feel undervalued. On the whole, people want to feel they make a difference. Staff do want to do a good job, but they need to feel supported in achieving this, or it is likely they will look elsewhere. Encouraging enterprise can help with this element by helping staff feel involved and that they are adding value. It can enable team members to utilize their skills and develop new ones. All of this can help them feel more appreciated.

Allowing staff to be enterprising can really help them feel

able to take control, make a difference, and make use of their skills. However, it's important that you not only encourage innovative thinking, but also allow staff to implement their ideas or they won't stay. Not only that, organisations who have a reputation for providing staff with a supportive and encouraging environment are more likely to attract high calibre applicants for vacancies within the organisation. Of course, this means that if you don't support and encourage enterprise, you will struggle to recruit staff who value such opportunities.

Case study

An organisation I worked with found that over time, their good staff had left. On reflection, they realised they had not encouraged or enabled staff to be enterprising or innovative, and indeed the staff who had left went to work for organisations that were more enterprising. In fact, many had left for their competitors. These competitors were then getting even stronger, building their teams of forward-thinking staff.

Now left playing catch-up to their competitors, this organisation started to realise the very skills they needed to be more enterprising were the skills they hadn't valued in their staff who had left.

Pride and connection

When employees talk about their employer with less than complementary words, I often ask them, "Are you proud of your employer, what it sells or provides, and are you proud of what you do and how you behave?" You see, if you are not proud of what you do and who you work for, it's hard to feel connected and willing to go out of your way to help that organisation become better. In effect, a poor employer who doesn't care about the business or their employees ends up with staff who don't care, no matter who they recruit in.

If you are not proud of your business and employees as the leader of your team or organisation, then it is likely your staff will feel the same. If you don't care, why should they? Staff who do care end up leaving to find an employer who cares as much as the individual does. Then you are just left with those who aren't bothered or can't even be bothered to look for a new opportunity.

Case study

A friend said to me, "It's easy for you to be proud of your teenagers. I'm not proud of mine." Wow, I thought. I was surprised and replied, "But you must be proud of your children, everyone is surely?" She pointed out to me that whilst she loved her children, she wasn't proud of them, stating that it's hard to be proud of children who sit on the sofa, watching re-runs on the television, eating pizza and drinking energy drinks. "Your children do things," she said. "They are trying their best to achieve."

Her belief was that it was hard to be proud of someone who wasn't bothered to put in the effort to even try to do something with their lives. I asked her, "Won't you try to help them change?" But her view was that she had spoken to them, offered them her support and ideas, and even tried to encourage, cajole, and bribe them — now it was down to them. If they couldn't be bothered to have pride in themselves, neither could she.

As the leader of her household, she needed to start encouraging her children to take more pride in their achievements, however small. As the leader of your organisation, you also need to help staff see the value they add and encourage them to take pride in their work. If you are not proud of their work, how can they be?

Personal commitment

When staff disengage and can't be bothered, it's often because their managers and leaders have also disengaged. However, some employers do all they can to provide their staff members with opportunities, and offer them care and support, yet in return there is no personal commitment from the employee. You need to be aware that just because you care and have pride in the work you do and in your organisation, it doesn't mean that everyone else does.

If you have staff who are always negative and sceptical about new ideas or opportunities, they can contaminate others. Just like a bad apple in a barrel, employees with poor attitudes can cause others to have similar attitudes. Instead, encourage those with more positive ideas to develop a personal commitment to making things happen and rise to the top. By supporting and encouraging positive staff members, it is often possible to foster a generally more positive workplace for all staff.

There are, of course, cases where staff who see possible difficulties are considered as negative. Be aware, there is a difference between people who are negative all the time, particularly when it comes to implementing change, and those who are negative about a given idea for a specific reason. Staff who are able and willing to highlight areas of concern about an idea that needs further work should be supported and encouraged.

> **Developing stretchy staff**
>
> When staff members do not want to make a personal commitment and are not proud of what they do, it can be because of laziness or disinterest. However, it can also be because of their previous experience. Maybe they feel that the employer let them down in the past, treated them unfairly, or didn't provide the level of support they felt they deserved. Staff who feel let down by an employer they once respected can struggle to reconnect. Understanding this and helping them to change their mind-set is often the first step on the path to staff engagement.

In reality, you will always have some staff who are resistant to change. Many "negative" people just need additional support and information to improve, but others may never adapt. In the end, staff with constant negative attitudes are best re-assigned or removed from the situation. Whilst it may not always be easy to do so, the consequences of them remaining and affecting the progress of the organisation can be much more of a problem, and affect many more people.

In general, staff have to *want* to help the organisation become successful. They must want to help because they are proud of the organisation and want to see it move on to even bigger and better things. Equally, they need to love what they do and the people they provide services or products to (the customer). They must feel they should do their best to help those people even more by giving them better quality products and services. Staff who demonstrate this commitment are more engaged with their employer and their future plans.

We don't have disengagement here, thank you

At the moment, you might believe that your staff are disengaged because of the way they respond to requests. When asked to do something different or new, do your staff say, "We don't do that here" or "We don't offer that service here"? If so, have you considered that they might not feel comfortable doing the task and are just trying to avoid it? Although they may come across as disengaged, is their "I can't" actually a result of their previous experience or a lack of confidence?

Your role is to help staff members see what they could achieve, rather than what they don't feel able to achieve. To help them feel that it's safe to give things a try, you as leader need to offer them support in their endeavours. To change from a "We don't do that / I don't do that" culture to one of "We'll / I'll give it a try", then you need to be supportive and trusting of your staff.

Developing stretchy staff

To reframe the views of your staff, start asking them questions in a different way. For example, imagine you work in a dentist practice and you ask your staff to try to sell a range of electric toothbrushes. Your staff might respond, "I don't think we should do that because our customers wouldn't like it."

Instead, you could ask your staff, "What do you think would happen if you offered customers a range of toothbrushes for sale?" or "What challenges do you see in offering a range of toothbrushes for sale?" This could open up an opportunity for staff to voice their concerns without giving "no" as a response.

Rather than giving staff the opportunity to just say no, ask them to consider what they could do and how they could improve things. Help them develop their own ideas to add value or bring in additional income. Staff find it harder to say no to their own ideas, while they can easily dismiss your ideas.

Don't forget that your aim is to develop staff who are willing to stretch outside their comfort zone. If they are anxious at the prospect of selling for the first time, then acknowledge their concerns and support them with appropriate learning opportunities.

Self-motivated to achieve

Some people seem to be self-motivated. Willing to try, willing to give things a go. Others need to be prompted, encouraged, or even forced to take action. However, some workplaces inadvertently quash this self-motivation when staff feel that their motives are questioned and their willingness is seen as overstepping the mark. Aim to be supportive and encourage your staff members to consider the implications through discussions.

Collaborative working

Enterprise is often considered to be about an individual taking action. But for enterprise in an organisation, collaborative working is hugely beneficial. This means encouraging your staff to come up with solutions together, and implementing those ideas as a group by sharing their skills, knowledge, and experience. In other words, staff need to support each other. It's much easier to battle on together when things seem impossible compared to when you are working alone. Also, by working together, the blame culture is reduced as everyone is involved in the idea.

Consider how your team could work if they all communicated better, shared skills and ideas, and supported each other in order to develop enterprising solutions.

Measuring staff engagement

Most human resources departments think that staff engagement is something they can and should measure. I know one company who sent their staff an employee engagement questionnaire with 150 questions in it! Wouldn't staff be disengaged just filling in the questionnaire? What's wrong with good old-fashioned discussions? The more you talk with your staff members as a leader or manager, the more you can gauge their level of engagement. This is about trust, honesty, and it feeling right for you and your team.

In larger organisations, you may feel the need to have standard and structured ways of measuring engagement. I suggest keeping things much simpler using just a few questions, or consider other options to check whether staff engagement is improving. Here are some measurable things to look out:

- staff turnover decreasing
- absenteeism and sickness rates lowering
- desire for people to join your company (your reputation as being a good place to work is getting out there into the world)
- returning customers and customers who refer you to others

- reduction in customer complaints, repeated problems, orders returned, or orders cancelled
- reduced costs and/or waste
- increased profits.

Building a business is not about KPIs

Key Performance Indicators (KPIs) can be a useful measurement tool and a way of setting work requirements in some cases. However, when it comes to enterprise, KPIs just don't work. This is because you would be suggesting that staff must carry out enterprising activities and will be measured against it. However, enterprise is born from seeing a need, rather than forcing someone to do something.

Let's say you set a KPI that a manager in your catering team must come up with a new idea or product that will increase the profits of the kitchen. If you set this as a KPI, the manager will quickly come up with any idea because you said they had to. However, it might not be the best idea. Instead, encourage enterprise as an activity, allowing things to develop organically from need and opportunities rather than forced targets.

Will enterprising staff expect big rewards?

Rewards are difficult when it comes to enterprise. Many organisations pay a "reward for ideas" bonus. So, if someone comes up with an idea that might help the organisation, they are financially rewarded. Usually, this reward is only paid if the idea is implemented successfully. However, the staff member often has no ownership of the idea and making it happen. If it works out, they just get a quick financial benefit, which on the whole isn't that large, but they have no sense of pride over the idea as they didn't make it happen. Will this small reward make them want to come up with another idea? Sticking your neck out and putting an idea forward is a big thing, and short-lived rewards may not be enough for your staff.

It's also possible that if people just see this as an exercise in "rewards for ideas", they will come up with ideas without really thinking them through, which could result in the idea being rejected. However, if the individual was incentivised to actually work on and develop their ideas, by giving the financial reward for the outcome of the idea or the benefit the idea brings in, their ideas may be more realistic and likely to succeed.

For many people, being involved in enterprising ways of working is not about financial rewards, but about feeling part of something bigger. It is about knowing that their work makes them part of the decision-making process and involved in the potential success of the organisation. Knowing that they are involved and informed can help some people feel more in control and less fearful of the unknown potential risks to their jobs, and for some people, this is reward enough. The rewards are longer term, and experience from enterprise activities stands staff in good stead for future opportunities, which is better than a temporary financial reward.

Case study

Ensure you are clear about what the rewards are, who will gain them, and when. One organisation I have heard of promised rewards for great ideas. When a staff member then came up with an idea that went on to make the organisation substantial profits, the person was disgruntled when they didn't get a bonus. At the year end, the team they worked in was each given a small bonus because one team member had come up with an idea. Yet only one person had come up with the idea and no one else on the team had any input. In trying to be fair, the organisation had left one staff member so disgruntled they left the organisation.

By being clearer from the beginning, the whole problem could have been avoided.

Beware, enterprise can be infectious!

Staff who are enterprising can often be the inspiration for developing a more creative and collaborative team and organisation. Anyone at any level can be enterprising. What's more, by encouraging staff who wish to work on more innovative projects to develop their own teams, they often become unexpected leaders. Similarly, those who join them may be people who you would never have considered if you had been selecting the team. The more that people are involved in enterprise, the more it reaps rewards, the more they will be inspired to do more enterprise. Beware, it is infectious and like anything, it needs to be nurtured and managed to ensure long-term success.

The importance of staff engagement and having good relationships between all levels of staff is clearly important to the general running of an organisation. If you wish to explore enterprise with your employees, then staff engagement becomes essential. Having a feeling of pride and connection to the organisation will lead to your employees feeling more willing to help the organisation develop and grow. Coupled with good relationships built on trust and open communication, your staff will feel more able to become involved in enterprise activities.

Summary

Staff engagement is key to enterprise development, and it is:

- A way of being, behaving, and working together as an organisation.
- A way of enabling staff to feel connected and involved.
- Based on trust and pride in your work.
- Difficult to measure and should not be about KPIs.
- Not always about rewarding ideas with money.

Chapter 5 –

Multi-level Communication – Joining up the Dots

"Accomplishing business growth needs clear and honest communication that everyone is part of."

Anyone who has worked within an organisation for any reasonable length of time will tell you that communication is key to the success of an organisation. In order to improve and move forward, you need good, clear, and honest communication. This is not just about talking, but really communicating to ensure everyone is learning and developing from the experiences they are having.

In this chapter, we'll explore:

- The multiple levels of communication: board, senior management, staff, and customers
- Putting customer need first
- Listening to staff and their ideas

Communication is the start of enterprise

Communication goes even deeper in enterprise development because it is the starting point to all things enterprise. Enterprise projects that have the best and most successful ideas are often those that see a need and fulfil that need. Discovering this need comes from looking, listening, and speaking to others. Most of all, it comes from understanding the customer and ensuring that the product or service completely meets that need. You can only make this happen by ensuring good communication.

Enterprises that are the most successful understand their abilities by having regular open communication. In addition, they know their limitations and abilities and the effect that these have on delivering what customers want. When staff know their own abilities and the abilities of those around them, it ensures that they only promise what they are capable of, and are capable of delivering what is promised. At the same time, they understand the organisation's abilities and desires to move forward. In short, staff who are kept well-informed can connect all the dots and create enterprise based on customer need, the abilities of the team, and the overall desire and drive to be successful.

This requires constant feedback, discussion, and communication at all levels of the organisation, as well as external communication with shareholders, stakeholders, banks, and regulatory bodies, as well as an awareness of the marketplace. Or in other words, multi-level communication. Let's look at these different levels for a moment:

Enterprise Within™

- The board need to keep all levels informed of their plans and desires to move the organisation forward. This will enable everyone to feed in the right ideas and consider how they can help.

- The board need to listen to ideas being submitted from the senior team and staff members as well as keeping an eye on their own customers' needs and other possible customers.

- The senior team need to let the board know what they are struggling with, how they can develop the organisation, and the skillset of themselves and their teams.

- The senior team need to let the staff members know about future plans so they can feed in ideas and know how to help.

- The senior team need to listen to customer needs direct from customers and via the staff members.

The Board | **The Senior Team**
The Customers | **The Staff**

- Everyone should be listening to the customers.

- Everyone needs to speak to the customers about their needs.

- Everyone should be considering what future needs the customers will have.

- Everyone should be listening to and speaking to people outside the business including the competition so they know what to consider next.

- The staff members need to be listening out for information from the customers.

- Staff need to use the information they get from day-to-day activities with the information recieved from the senior team and board to help develop ideas.

- Staff need to feed back ideas and information to the senior team when and where appropriate to the board.

[95]

Putting the customers at the core of your business communication

The more you listen to your customers' needs and use that information, the more you will improve the business, whether it's improving the quality of service or the product itself, or adding additional services that have been requested or seem to be in need. This is "customer-led growth". You are looking to grow and move forward based on what your customers are requesting, rather than on what you believe is needed.

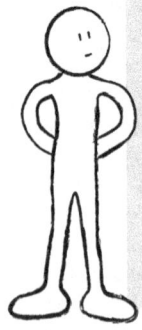

Consider this...

If you work within a statutory organisation, charity, or government-funded body, your customers may be mixed, such as service users and other organisations. In this case, it is also possible to hold customer feedback panels or sessions where you can enable service users to feed in their ideas to help with enterprise projects. For example, a housing association could ask tenants to work with them on considering what new services they would like added to a town, estate, or area. Or a charity may work with its benefactors to improve the quality of its provision or increase income generation. This involvement can help ensure long-term buy-in from those who are already connected with your organisation.

Asking customers or service users for their ideas does not mean that you have to give them everything they are asking for. It is possible that sometimes the customers' needs are not aligned with your abilities or business purpose and you will have to accept you can't answer that need. It is all about responding to feedback and listening to customers to ensure your business is moving in the right direction for you and the customers you already serve.

Do you mean we need a customer survey?

"Ah!" you say. "Fantastic, we can do a customer survey — that will give us customer-led growth." But unfortunately, this isn't enough as it will only give you a snapshot in time.

You can see from this example that by allowing staff time to have this this two-way communication, it enables you to really understand a situation and how it can be improved or rectified. Whilst this may take time, the long-term improvements can save time and increase customer satisfaction. It may not be possible to speak at length to people all the time, but ask staff to keep a note of regular similar conversations and situations. Whilst surveys and questionnaires can add value, don't forget to include the one-off conversations and verbal feedback during your decision-making processes.

Case study

Think of it like this. I come to my doctor's surgery and arrive to find the car park full. I park down the road and by the time I put a ticket on and walk back up the road, I'm late. The receptionist points this out and says I have missed my appointment and makes me feel really bad. But I end up waiting anyway. No one tells me the doctor is actually running late, so I just sit and wait. This ends up being a frustrating trip, which could easily have been handled better. I see the receptionist on the way out and ask whether it is possible to be told on the way in if the doctor is running late. She replies: "Well, you were late as well." True, but not helpful.

> Later on, I get a survey that asks for feedback about the surgery. One of the questions is about doctors running late, to which I tick 'Yes'. I also am asked about the receptionist's attitude. I score them low, based on my experience of that occasion, but not necessarily on other occasions. How helpful is that information? I would say not very. Instead, how much more helpful would it be if the receptionist had spoken to me and asked what could they do to help at the time? I could then suggest that when it's really busy, they could send a text or let me know when I book that it is a busy day with various clinics, or that the car park is likely to be full. This will help me decide to leave more time to find a parking space. They could also let me know when I arrive that the doctor is running late so I can decide whether I can wait or not.

Using information to develop a new approach or enterprising solution

By listening to customers and really discussing their needs, it is possible to implement customer-led growth. Once staff members have information about customers' or service users' needs, it is important that they have a way of taking that information and using it to benefit the organization and the people it serves.

How much authority do your staff have when it comes to taking the information and using it to make a decision? A decision that changes the experience of the individual and future clients? How much decision-making power do they actually have? How easy is it for them to discuss their ideas for improvement and ensure they are considered by others within the organisation?

You may want to set some parameters or ways in which staff can communicate these points. Equally, it is worth giving staff a level of empowerment that means they can make changes to give customers an improved experience. We have all experienced being in a shop or restaurant where we were unhappy with something and the person serving us tells us they don't have the authority to offer an alternative or a refund, and that they would have to ask the manager. It all seems a bit frustrating and unnecessary, doesn't it? It's so much better when the person serving apologises and offers to fix it right away, without the need to check with a more senior person.

Developing stretchy staff

Staff who feel they are trusted to make decisions and empowered to use their own initiative are more likely to feel involved and connected to the organisation. This in turn leads them to seek out other good quality ideas and opportunities, as they are aware they need to stretch themselves whilst accepting the need to be careful and avoid risk.

Don't worry that they will start to make decisions above their abilities and authority. By having open and honest conversations about things they will need to seek advice on, they are more likely to go to their managers automatically. It comes back to two-way trust and good, clear communication. Staff rarely implement ideas or decisions above their authority without checking first.

Listening to staff and their ideas

The more willing you are to listen to different ideas and the views of others, including your staff members, the more likely it is that your organisation will benefit from a new way of working and thinking. All problems have multiple solutions, and while shutting senior staff members away in boardrooms or at retreats may have worked in the past, is this the right way forward for your organisation now?

Research has shown that many new successful entrepreneurs came up with their business idea while working for their previous employer. They chose to leave because they found that their previous employer didn't listen to or encourage their ideas. Is this what you want for your organisation?

Developing stretchy staff

If your staff members are stretchy in the way they think and are involved in the work day in, day out, it's possible that they will have also worked in similar roles in other organisations or they may speak to their peers in other organisations. This means that if they are made aware of the problems, they might come up with a different solution, a new angle, or a different take on the problem. If they don't know you are dealing with the problem, they will never know that their ideas are required.

Miscommunication

When staff members have an idea but it isn't taken up or moved forward, it can often be down to miscommunication.

Managers and leaders may not have fully explained their interest in hearing such ideas, so the staff member never even comes forward and tells them. Alternatively, the staff member comes forward, but doesn't communicate the idea clearly enough. It's also possible that the staff member doesn't understand how their idea could fit into the overall business plan, so they don't link their idea into the organisational plan in a way that leaders and managers can see the benefits.

Miscommunication can, of course, happen the other way as well. Leaders and managers can poorly explain what they are looking for from staff members, or not fully explain how something will work. The most damaging miscommunication is not clearly explaining the aims and expectations of everyone in relation to enterprise.

Be sure you know what you want and why from your staff members, then communicate this to them clearly and check they understand. Make sure they know how they can work with you and benefit themselves, as well as the organisation.

Be willing and able to listen to staff when they talk through their failures. Help them to accept what went wrong, what they can learn from it, and how to let go and move on. Supportive communication that helps them learn and grow is vital in enterprise.

What staff need to know

In order to make a difference and support enterprise in your organisation, staff need to understand some fundamentals of business. They need to know about:

- Business models
- Taking a product or service to market
- Reaching customer expectations

- The need for systems and controls
- Developing measurable solutions
- Cost controls, waste, etc.
- Technology
- Anything else that makes your business work.

Which staff should I be listening to?

Well, all of them really. Any staff member could come up with a great idea. Staff who enjoy solving business problems and developing new ideas will often talk excitedly at meetings about their ideas. They will also seek out like-minded colleagues to help them form the ideas into solid business proposals, enabling them to be developed. But keep an eye out for staff who are not so vocal. They could have a well-considered idea that they feel unsure about talking about and fear drawing attention to themselves and their idea before it is fully considered. Often, these staff members never feel their idea is ready to be shared, or by the time they are ready, your competitors have also spotted the same opportunity.

Communication between teams

Specialisation and separation of teams and functions within an organisation can hinder communication. This means it's difficult to know about new ideas that are being considered and developed within different sections of the organisation. Having a central point where these ideas are considered can really help. This central point can link up ideas and help people form connections. Here, conversations can be held to see how ideas would support each other or where an idea may not currently be suitable.

Consider having regular enterprise meet-ups. Development days, learning sessions, and even mastermind groups can all help individuals share and work on their ideas. By pooling ideas and information, projects can be developed quicker and as the manager, you can keep abreast of all the ideas by dipping in and out of these sessions.

Summary

Good communication is vital to success, so you need to ensure good communication within your organisation by doing the following:

- Understand the communication required at all levels of the organisation.

- Listen to customers and use the information derived from them to develop new approaches or solutions.

- Listen to staff and their ideas, avoid miscommunication, and make sure staff know what they need to know.

Chapter 6 -

Customer-led Growth – More than Just What People Want

"Every organisation depends on its customer relationships, delivery is not just about today but yesterday, today, and every day from here on in."

Now your staff are communicating more and listening to the needs of customers, how can you be sure they are doing something with this knowledge? How can you ensure your staff are fully engaged with the business so they can help make it as stable as possible for the future? Ultimately, by listening to customers and really discussing their needs, it is possible to implement customer-led growth. For me, this should be at the heart of every enterprise: listening to and being led by your customers.

In this chapter, we'll look at:

- The delivery gap
- Seeing things from the customer's perspective
- Strategic scanning
- Touch points
- Setting yourself apart
- Being strategically responsive.

The delivery gap

Much of the time, there is a delivery gap between what the organisation believes it is delivering to clients and service users and what they believe they are receiving. You may think you are great because clients use your services, but it could be that they tolerate your poor customer service because you are cheap or local, or they feel they have no other option. Closing this delivery gap sounds much easier than it is in reality. First, you need to be aware of the gap, then understand what causes the gap, and finally know how to resolve the gap.

Is the gap in what you believe you deliver and what the client or service user receives? Is it about quality, price, or delivery of expectations? Is it about other areas of your business, such as reputation, the general experience of using your services, or the relationship side of the transaction process?

How to spot a delivery gap

To discover whether you have a delivery gap, you need to have clear and effective communication with your customers. Then you need to consider the information you have collated and use this along with knowledge about your business, expertise, staff, and abilities to discover a way of moving the business forward. This should be led by what your clients need, rather than what you believe they need and not necessarily what they believe they want.

It is important that you stand outside the organisation and see things from your client's side. To ensure you see things from a client's perspective, you may need to employ mystery shopper solutions or advisors with expertise in your sector. These can enable you to gain insights from an external person's perspective. If this isn't possible currently, then try walking through your customers' experience yourself and ask staff members to do the same. Try to be as objective as possible when doing this. These options can, of course, be combined with quality, well-run customer surveys or interviews. Indeed, the more you interact with these clients and really listen to them, the easier this will become.

Developing services and products that your clients are happy with and need will make it easier to encourage them to come back for more. Furthermore, staff members will become aware of what customers need and can ensure their needs are met. The more engaged staff members are with the organisation, what it can do and offer, and how it needs to grow, the easier it will be for them to provide customers with the right level of service that makes them happy, while also benefiting the organisation.

If this seems way too simple, then you're forgetting that it's not about a knee-jerk reaction to customer wants and offering something just because customers want it. Instead, it's about understanding customers' real needs and feeding these into the bigger picture—where they inform decisions rather than being the complete solution, and where you select elements that suit the way the organisation is developing. Enterprise Within™ requires the customer to be at the centre of plans and ideas, and you taking customer relations to another level. On this level, staff listen to customers and consider their additional needs in order to inform the organisation of opportunities to expand and grow.

As an organisation, you should be there to serve your clients, not just to meet your targets, KPIs, or personal goals. These are a measurement tool for your own performance, yet we often use them to measure success. Success should be an organisation that is sustainable and growing, and has satisfied customers or service users.

Strategic scanning

Engaged staff care about the bigger picture and not just their pay packet and KPIs. When staff feel involved and are aware of the aims of the organisation, it is easier for them to keep an eye out for ideas and possibilities. This is often referred to as "strategic scanning".

You need to always be on the lookout for ideas, considering what customers need, will need, and possibly will want in the future. In addition, you need to keep an eye on the competition and ways in which other organisations (both within your area of work and outside) are developing and providing customers with solutions. For example, if you make use of online booking systems for a restaurant, you can then start to ask what else can I book online, like haircuts or dental appointments? Can the same be done in your industry sector or business type? Once people have accessed a service or product in a more convenient way, they will want to do the same for other organisations they use.

Keeping abreast of new ideas, delivery services, and options are key to developing for the future. Encouraging your staff to be aware of changes, developments, and new technology can all be part of your strategic scanning. In addition, it is important to be aware off other changes that may impact on the way people access your services or expect to buy your products. As things around you change—locally, nationally, and worldwide—you need to consider the implications for your organisation.

Developing stretchy staff

An opticians decides to listen to what customers need in order to add additional services, and they find that their customers are looking to purchase things as diverse as paint and vegetables. However, that doesn't mean they are going to start selling paint and vegetables in the corner of the shop next to the glasses and contact lenses! But, they also kept hearing customers talk about the difficulties of getting to the nearest city to access care or support with their hearing aid, which they thought could be worth exploring as a similar service to their current offering.

After research, they discovered they can receive training and offer an element of hearing aid care. This is stretchy thinking, but seems like a sensible move as the opticians wants to become a place where people can discuss healthcare requirements, rather than just a place to buy glasses. By offering a similar service with hearing aids, more people will enter the shop and the business will build a stronger care support brand.

Innovation and Idea Generation

Identify a need.

Consider whether you have the ability to meet the need.

If you attempt to meet the need, will it be good for the organisation? Now or in the future?

Are you meeting the needs of your customers?

Strategic scanning needs to be about being responsive to changing needs and altering marketplaces and being aware of the longer-term vision and aims of the organisation. These need to be considered in line with the customer needs so that when opportunities arise, it is easier to know whether they are worth considering and developing further. Organisational agility is a key element of enterprise and it links back to being aware of the need and knowing whether you have the skills and resources to respond to that need. It also requires knowing whether it is sensible for the longer-term sustainability of the organisation to engage in the opportunity.

Agility in your business

So, it's vital that your business is agile. However, agile does not mean sloppy or jumping from one thing to another. Just as running a lean business doesn't mean scrimping or cutting corners. Running an agile organisation means you are able to respond to changing needs and know how to implement those changes successfully. It is about being aware of your customer needs, listening to them, learning from them, and considering the environment in which you work. This means you can plan for what your customers need today and tomorrow.

Having an agile business requires knowledge. You need to be fully aware of the skills you already have within the organisation, even those not currently being utilised. You also need to understand what capacity you have to expand, retract, and alter the course of your work so that you can make changes quickly and efficiently when the need arises.

Organisations who wish to be more agile need to combine the flexibility of their organisation and the staff within it, as well as having the ability to be strategically responsive to customer need. In order to do this, you need to ensure your team members have the skills they need. The best solution here is to embrace a learning organisation approach.

Developing enterprise from the customer's point of view

It is possible to not only think like a customer and what they need, but also involve the customers in developing enterprising solutions. Consider how you could get your customers involved. How early on in the decision-making process could you involve them? Would they be interested in trialling new ideas for you? Could they provide feedback when you are testing ideas? If you have their feedback and views, this will help develop the idea in line with customer needs. By having them involved early on, they can influence products and services they really need or want. In addition, they are more likely to purchase from you and tell others about you.

Stakeholders, the third sector, and not-for-profits

On the whole, organisations such as community groups, charities, and government-funded agencies tend to be set up to deliver what is needed and more often than not, what they are paid to deliver. Their focus is on doing the best possible with the resources available. However, running an enterprise idea or project is different, as it must add value and not simply serve a need that has funding or pre-agreed income attached. Now you need to find an idea that people will buy.

Your customers will now have to decide whether they are willing to pay you for your new idea, unlike previously where they accessed your services or products for free or at a reduced cost. For example, perhaps you are a charity who has offered support to your local community including training courses that have been fully funded in the past, so your attendees have not paid anything to train. However, you may now be looking at bringing in an income by charging for your courses. This will require a mind-set shift around how you promote them, who you promote them to, and the level of service you offer. You will now need to convince current service users of the value of your courses so that they will pay, or you will need to find new customers.

Any organisation that hasn't previously been involved in enterprise and now needs to do so must involve their customers and stakeholders so they fully understand what they need to offer. In addition, it helps to get buy-in for these new ideas early on. That way, you can gauge from customers how they would like these services or products delivered, what their expectations are around price and quality, and how they wish to access them.

In the example of selling courses, you could speak to your potential clients about their levels of need so you can understand the demand. In addition, you can ask them about their views on the type, duration, and price of the courses. The more clarity you have over people's needs, the more likely it is that your enterprise project will be a success.

Stakeholder feedback of non-core services

Getting stakeholder feedback on your non-core service is different to getting feedback on your core services. For example, when you have had a funding cut and ask stakeholders for their view on how to approach your core services, it's very different to asking for their opinion on developing new enterprise projects. Cutting back on services in a local council after government cuts requires stakeholder review, but these views can be very emotionally charged. Stakeholders' ideas of what should and shouldn't be cut are based on their experiences and opinions, not necessarily on the reality of the budgets involved. In enterprise projects, you are asking stakeholders for their views on accessing different services or products, or similar services but in a different way.

When speaking to stakeholders, ensure it's clear how these enterprise projects fit into the overall picture of your normal core work. Otherwise, they may be worried it will affect the core purpose of your organisation. Any enterprise idea must fit within the core ethos and values of your organisation, and add to its long-term stability. Then this needs to be communicated with stakeholders.

Touch points - focusing on delivery

When a customer or client connects with a business in any way, we call it a touch point. This can be an actual, physical touch, such as going into a shop or office or picking up your product. A touch point can also mean virtually connecting via social media or your website, seeing information about you in a magazine or newspaper, or even hearing about your work second-hand.

It is important to consider these touch points and how good those experiences are for your customers and potential customers. The more an organisation considers their customer touch points and general experiences and needs, the more successful they are likely to be, much more than if they had focused on their internal processes or KPIs.

Your customers often have a choice to use you or not—they also have a voice and can use it to the detriment of your organisation. If you provide a service where a customer doesn't have choice, remember that they still have a voice. And they can use this voice to make your job much harder than it needs to be. If customers' current experience of using your services or products is poor, then you will get poor quality information from your customers when it comes to looking at growth innovation by expanding. This is because their ideas, feedback, and views will be tarnished by previous bad touch points.

Touch points include customer care, but are also much more than someone's direct experience with your organisation. Don't be fooled into thinking that by training your staff in customer care, this is enough to ensure good touch points. Everyone is providing customer care training these days. You need to find even more to set your organisation apart and ensure you are remembered by your customers.

What sets you apart

I'm not suggesting here that you start to identify your Unique Selling Point (USP). Many of the organisations I work with don't really have a USP in its true sense. If you provide a service or a product but you know people could access similar elsewhere, then you need to stop worrying about what makes you unique and consider whether there are things your business can do that would set you apart.

Many things can set you apart so customers can see the benefit and will continue to use your organisation's offerings. Consider areas such as service, quality, flexibility, fast turnaround, understanding of customers' needs, language needs, availability of services, quality of your staff, etc.

This means that customer service needs to be an organisational default. It's not just about retaining customers, keeping them happy, and being nice to them, but about really being grateful for them choosing your business. This means you really need to listen to what they need and how you can help them. You need to ensure your offerings suit their needs and work with them so they keep using your services or products.

Keep customers at the heart of everything you do

An enterprising organisation has its customers and potential customers at the very heart of everything it does. This means it's important that you really understand customers and their expectations. As well as this, it's also vital that all staff members understand why the organisation is there and what it needs to achieve in order to be sustainable.

Allowing staff to be enterprising in the way they work can take many forms at many levels. For example, it can be enabling them to respond to customer needs and requests with minimal fuss, such as making changes to orders without adding an admin fee or upgrading a regular customer because it's their birthday. Of course, it could be more about developing new offers, products, and services. Whatever the staff are looking at doing, make sure the customers are kept at the heart of all decisions and plans.

Case study

Having run out of business cards, I contacted my printers and asked for them to print me some new ones. However, I needed them urgently as I was travelling away with work. "Not a problem," the sales guy said, "I'll get them sent to where you are going." But I needed them at the meeting I had on the way there as well. "Not a problem," he said, "I'll get them sent to the first venue." I was worried I would only be there a few hours, but he was sure they would be there.

When I got to my client, there was a parcel waiting for me with a note inside saying *Hope these got to you okay. I have also sent more to your next venue.* Sure enough, when I reached my second venue, there was another parcel with cards inside. This time, the note read *Hope you got this morning's parcel. If not, here are some more cards. If you got both parcels, that's great but we only charged you for one.*

A simple and not-that-expensive solution made sure I was a happy customer. This simple, customer-focused, stretchy, and enterprising solution made me a raving fan of the company.

Tune your staff into customers' needs and organisational gain

You probably talk about customer care a lot, and no doubt your staff have been trained in customer service and looking after customer needs. But much of this focuses on the relationship and communication between staff members and customers in what you already provide. To encourage a more enterprise-focused organisation, staff members need to see the relationship between customers and organisational growth, profits, and sustainability.

Your role is to encourage them to see what more can be done to ensure customer needs are met and that the organisation benefits in the long run. If you speak to an entrepreneur running their own business, customers are hugely important, but not to the detriment or exclusivity of the organisation. You need your staff to see the links between customers, profits, and their job with you. Therefore by helping them to develop an understanding about how the business functions and grows, they can better understand how to add value.

Summary

Enterprise is about customer-led growth, but this doesn't just mean blindly providing your customers with everything they want.

- Discover your delivery gap — what you think you're delivering and what you're actually delivering.
- See things from the customer's perspective.
- Ensure you're strategically scanning — looking for suitable future opportunities based on customer need.
- Focus on delivery and your customer touch points.
- Set yourself apart by understanding your organisation and what you are offering.
- Be strategically responsive.
- Keep customers at the heart of everything you do.

PART FOUR:

Enabling Enterprise Within™ *in Your Organisation*

Enterprise Within™

Chapter 7 –

Learning Ladder to Growth

"Give yourself a competitive advantage through sharing knowledge and learning in your teams – build a learning organisation."

As learning and development is a key element of enterprise, it's vital that your organisation embraces learning at its very core. To encourage your teams to be enterprising, they will need opportunities to try new ideas and learn as they go. It's likely that your team will need to gain some basic information around enterprise and business as a starting point. In addition, they need to learn from their failures, be able to try again, and refine ideas until they work – building their resilience to failure and knowledge of building a successful enterprise.

Perhaps more importantly, the organisation itself needs to encourage and enable learning and enterprise activities to take place in a secure and encouraging way. This requires learning to be at the core of the organisation's aims. Learning for enterprise development can be considered as a ladder, where each step moves the organisation nearer to the end goal of having a more collaborative team. This enables enterprise to take place in a safe and structured way.

In this chapter, we'll look at:

- The steps on the learning ladder to enterprise success
- Encouraging curious and proactive staff

- The importance of action learning
- Developing resilience
- Team growth and knowledge transfer
- Supporting learning activities in your organisation

Organisational growth through enterprise requires a culture of sharing and learning. Sharing ideas and supporting each other can be exciting and enlightening. It enables individuals to share ideas and experiences, and learn from each other. An organisation that embraces a culture of continuous learning is referred to as "a learning organisation". This style of learning suits any organisation that is aiming to embrace an enterprising way of working.

What is a learning organisation?

A learning organisation is one that looks to constantly transform itself and develop by engaging its employees in learning. There has been much research into the concept of "knowledge transfer" and sharing learning experiences in the workplace. The research confirms that by respecting each other's abilities and experiences, we can learn and grow from each other within an organisation. Transferring knowledge within an organisation gives it a competitive advantage, particularly when learning is across different business units or areas.

The learning ladder to developing an enterprising organisation

Anyone immersed in the world of enterprise will tell you that enterprise is about learning. Learning about your own abilities, learning from the process of trying things out, and learning from other people around you. Your organisation may already promote the idea of knowledge sharing and embedding learning and review into its day-to-day running.

Enterprise Within™

Or you may have a long way to go to encourage learning amongst your teams. Whichever is the case, it is worth understanding how the various elements of learning link together like rungs on a ladder.

Embrace a Learning Organisation

Show staff how learning is a complete organisational development tool, not just something for an individual.

Support Learning

Provide ways for staff to learn. Encourage them to not only learn but use what they have learnt.

Encourage Knowledge Transfer

Knowledge is more beneficial to an organisation when shared. Encourage structured sharing of knowledge.

Develop Resilience

Resilient people accept that failure is part of life and can bounce back. Help staff learn how to do this.

Action Learning

Enable staff to learn through activities. Provide them with a way to try, review, and reflect so they can progress and improve.

Enable Proactive Staff

Provide staff with the structure and levels of empowerment needed to be more proactive in their approach.

Fuel Curiosity

Help staff to develop a curious mind so they look out for ideas and opportunities they can bring back to your organisation.

≫ Innovation and Idea Generation ≪

Fuel curiosity

As children, we learnt about the world around us often because our curiosity led us to explore, ask questions, test things out, and understand how things work, taste, feel, and so forth. That curiosity and desire to understand is needed again when we are talking about enterprise. Having a curious mind will lead you to question whether a product or service can be improved upon, altered, or offered in a different way. By being curious, you will look at what others are offering and wonder whether it's something you can replicate. Of course, curiosity can lead you to find a new solution to a problem and in doing so, can help you develop a new product or service never previously considered.

Staff need to be encouraged to be curious. Invite them to ask questions, consider alternative approaches, and discover whether the current solutions work for your customers and provide the organisation with the best options for growth.

Enable proactive staff

To develop a more enterprising workforce, you need staff who are both curious and proactive. So, you have to encourage your teams to be proactive in seeking out ideas and solutions, in their own development, and in the growth of the organisation.

In being proactive, staff need to stop expecting things to be handed to them on a plate. So instead of telling them which courses or events to attend, ask them to bring you ideas of things they feel would benefit them and the organisation. Inform them that it doesn't mean they can go to any event or training course they wish, but via discussion, you can agree on the ones most suited to them and the organisation's bottom line.

This encourages them to see learning and development as something they can take active control of. That it's something for the mutual benefit of the individual and the organisation. Learning should be about being curious, and discovering things that can move the organisation forward.

Help staff develop a curiosity for ideas and information as well as knowing how to feed back into their organisation. It is important they can see how to share information back into the organisation as a whole.

Your role as a leader is to encourage staff to be curious and then to take action.

Developing stretchy staff

A staff member attends a conference around online marketing. Whilst much of the information was useful in their day-to-day job within the marketing team, they also attended a talk about customer data and how to use it more effectively. Having taken some notes, they then find the right person in the organisation to share the information with. This is a more proactive approach than deciding "this talk is nothing to do with me" and switching off.

Get active with action learning

No doubt, it's clear to you as a leader that learning is important. But there are many different types of learning. To develop a more enterprising way of thinking amongst your team, you need to help individuals take part in action learning or "learning by doing". In other words, experimenting, trying things out, and evaluating how they go before moving forward.

This type of learning can help people move forward when facing problems. It also provides them with a bank of experiences to draw upon at any time when making decisions now or in the future. Much of the decision-making in enterprise is about weighing up the pros and cons, then going with *what feels right* based on previous experiences. But this can only be done if you have those previous experiences.

Action learning is about going through real-life or simulated experiences and then reflecting on all aspects of the experience in order to learn from it. This reflection needs to be done in a planned way with feedback from others when appropriate and a review of other options.

For example, a small team decide to change the ordering process for clients. After much discussion, they decide on the new process and select a small number of clients to try the new process. Without action learning, they could blindly try it out, decide it works well for those clients, and then implement it across all clients without any alterations. With action learning, however, they will discuss the different stages as a group and consider their experiences, those of their clients, and any feedback they have gained. This can be fed back to a mentor or manager who can help them consider whether it needs any alterations or a completely different approach. Changes can be made without anyone feeling their idea is being questioned. The altered approach can be re-tested and reviewed until the idea is deemed suitable for further roll-out or not a viable option currently, if ever.

Action learning can be carried out by an individual, although it is more commonly carried out with a mentor or external person to facilitate the reflection. It is also a great way to encourage collaborative learning and can be carried out through group action learning sessions, also referred to as "learning sets" or "mastermind groups". When developing a more enterprising culture, it is worth promoting collaborative learning as it avoids repeating similar mistakes and ensures a wealth of knowledge is available to focus on finding suitable solutions.

Collaborative learning

Working in teams or groups can enable us to share learning experiences. In addition, we can gain ideas and knowledge from others as we complete a task. In days gone by, learning was offered by sitting with or working with someone more experienced. This was often referred to as "sitting with Nelly", which was developed in the industrial revolution. The downside of this style of learning is that by learning from one person in the traditional "apprentice and master" style, you not only learn the good, but also the bad or incorrect.

By working in larger groups, collaborative learning allows all team members to question and consider various ideas, experiences, and points of view. Collaborative learning is also more likely to have an element of reflection, as some of us are naturally reflectors more than others. It is usual for someone in the group to be the one who asks questions that will encourage everyone to reflect. Such questions include:

- What problems did we encounter and how did we overcome them?
- What resources would we need to make this work on a bigger scale?
- How do we all feel about the solution we adopted now we have tried it?
- In what ways could we approach this differently?
- Moving forward, how could we improve this?

- What difficulties could we envisage in gaining buy-in to this idea from all staff?

Of course, collaborative learning also means there is a mix of experiences, ideas, knowledge, and opportunities. When trying out enterprising ideas, a lot of it is about knowing who you can go to for help. By having a team of people, your network of supporters is as valuable as your team's wealth of ability.

Developing resilience

Enterprising activities can be hugely valuable, but can also be hugely frustrating. At times, staff will be working hard on an idea, finding a solution, or breaking into a new area of work only to discover they have made a mistake, the idea isn't quite right, or more work needs to be done. Sometimes, a return to the drawing board is required. In order to not give up or continue on the wrong path, staff need a level of resilience. Being resilient means having the ability to dig a bit deeper and try again, rather than giving up. This is often referred to as "a mind-set for growth".

Help staff develop a mind-set for growth

A mind-set is an established set of attitudes or beliefs held by someone about an area of their ability. For example, I may have the attitude that as I once tried windsurfing at 16 and wasn't very good at it, that I don't have the ability to do it now. If someone suggests going windsurfing and I have a fixed mind-set, I would say, "No thanks, I'm no good at windsurfing". Whereas if I have an open mind-set, I would say "Hmm, windsurfing. I tried that once. It didn't go so well, but if someone teaches me, I'll try it again". I may find that I can do it this time. This is about being willing to stretch yourself outside your comfort zone and think "if I tried it, maybe I could learn".

People with a fixed mind-set will tell themselves they are no good at something to avoid a challenge or failure, or looking dumb, which holds them back from achieving it. If you have a fixed mind-set, you perceive that your talent and intelligence is what it is. Those with an open mind-set understand that their abilities, talents, and intelligence can be developed through effort, practice, and trying. They also accept that sometimes they may fail, but by learning from failure and trying again with new-found information, experience, and examples, they can grow and move forward.

You already know that you shouldn't be swayed by the opinion of others, especially when people say, "You will never achieve that" when you haven't yet even tried. Or indeed swayed by your own internal conversation within yourself, "You will never be able to do that, stop now". This is your mind-set and what you may not realise is that your mind-set could already be affecting your possible outcome. By thinking *I can't* or believing *I won't be able to*, your negative thought patterns are likely to lead you to failure, not success. So how do you change the mind-set of your team?

Changing a poor mind-set

If you encourage your staff to work together with an open mind-set, to be stretchy, it will enable them to see that failure is an opportunity to improve. They'll see that they can move forward by trying things, accepting they may not be right first time, knowing that it is not necessary to blame others, and using it to learn and gain new ideas and new experiences. This in turn will help your organisation to move forward and grow.

In this way, we look to learn from mistakes and grow together. Think about what you could do to deliver even more to your clients if only you and your team believed they could. Changing your individual and team mind-set or an organisational mind-set requires a development-based environment like what's seen within a learning organisation.

For your team to develop and help the organisation grow, they will need to become a resilient team. Individually, they may feel like giving up or think they don't have the skills required, but as a team they can learn and grow together and become stronger in order to master their challenges and help move the organisation forward.

To become more resilient, they need to accept that to grow, they have to try new things and some of those things may not work out. However, through feedback and reviewing all areas of work, the successes and failures will enable them to develop more knowledge and skills, and therefore more resilience.

An enterprising person is always searching for improvements, implementing them, and making the best of opportunities to ensure the long-term sustainability of their work and their organisation. To do this, they need to be aware of how to grow as an individual and what elements they need to work on to develop their skills. It's also very important that they have self-awareness of their abilities, as well as their failings. That way, they can see that whilst they may not be perfect, they certainly have skills that can benefit the organisation. By knowing what you are good at and understanding that we all have failures, it is easier for staff to be resilient. It's about having an ability to bounce back, rather than giving up when things are not going your way.

Bounce-back-ability

One of the entrepreneurial traits that staff need to embrace is "bounce-back-ability". This is because sometimes when we stretch ourselves, things can go wrong. You don't want your staff to just give up at that point. By having bounce-back-ability, you accept that things go wrong, learn from your mistakes, and try again. This is what makes an individual truly enterprising.

As enterprise often involves dealing with new experiences, it's important to support your staff to develop problem-solving skills. Help them evaluate what went wrong and how the mistakes can be avoided in the future, so they can bounce back from their problems quickly.

Resilience in your organisation

Developing resilience within your organisation will ensure that staff members always seek to improve and grow. This is done by encouraging the whole organisation to consider moving forward through effort, rather than accepting limits.

Not every idea we consider is fully formed and developed. To embrace enterprise in your workplace, everybody needs to be willing to accept failure, learn from it, and move on without feeling the need to keep reviewing and reliving ideas that were not successful, or trying to make a bad idea work. In short, failure shouldn't be seen as a negative experience, but as a step closer to achieving the aim.

This means that you as a leader need to support staff by avoiding blame or a culture where there is a fear of failure. Encourage your staff to embrace failure as a way of learning by considering what positives they can take from an experience, what learning points they've gained, and what they need to avoid next time. Then, help them look at the next step or idea so they can move on from the negative experience, knowing you have confidence in their ability to get it right—it just wasn't right this time.

By embracing this learning style in an organisation, staff

will see that it's okay to try and to fail. They will see that the most important element is sharing experiences and learning together to avoid repeating failed attempts or blame.

Whatever decision is made regarding whether to try again or stop a project, remember that communicating with staff about the decision is important. You must avoid staff members jumping to conclusions. It is easy to feel hurt or rejected when your idea is stopped from progressing. Learning why an idea has not moved forward will help staff accept decisions and bounce back with other ideas in the future.

Encourage knowledge transfer

Learning, in my opinion, is a continual thing, and it should happen in a variety of ways and be shared for the greater good of the organisation. In the past, staff training was organised by the Human Resources department, and larger organisations had a training department or learning co-ordinators. Their job was to identify learning needs and develop suitable programs, courses, and events to match that need. Whilst some learning still happens this way, we also know that there are many more ways that learning can take place such as coaching, mentoring both from senior to junior staff members and junior members to senior members, plus peer-to-peer learning.

A learning organisation is one that is continually developing and learning through its activities and those of its staff. It reviews experiences and learns from them in order to develop and move forward. This involves a way of working that can help with problem solving, learning from organisational experiences, learning from the experiences of team members, and transferring knowledge quickly amongst team members. This type of continuous learning and sharing fits well with the concept of being more enterprising.

A learning organisation provides a perfect way of solving problems, introducing new solutions, and trying out new ideas. To develop a learning organisation, you should consider how you and your employees learn from previous experiences. Provide staff with opportunities to reflect on experiences and learn from those activities. It is your role to ensure that the organisation is continuously developing and moving forward, rather than making the same or similar mistakes as before.

Sharing knowledge and learning together rather than in silos is vital to develop a more enterprising culture within your organisation. By sharing knowledge and learning experiences, positive steps, and failures, we can help others avoid similar mistakes, resolve problems, and share ideas to move forward when we encounter difficulties.

Only by sharing can others find out what you need help with or spot an opportunity you may have missed. A learning organisation needs its staff members to share learning at all levels, including personal experiential learning and learning from external sources, such as events, books, etc.

Holding back knowledge can be detrimental to an organisation and each other's development. For a true organisational learning environment, there needs to be a desire to share and see others succeed — not a harsh competitive environment built on mistrust and the need to hold back knowledge to retain power over others.

Sharing knowledge within your organisation can provide you with a competitive advantage by bringing various elements together to make decisions with full knowledge of the matter rather than half-truths or partial information.

Support learning

To ensure that staff involved in enterprise are suitably equipped to be successful, you need to provide them with the tools and support to learn. As individuals, we are constantly learning. It is not surprising that most learning happens when we try something new, as we must either develop new skills or alter our way of thinking or behaving in order to be successful at the task.

As adults, much of our learning comes from reflection — looking back at a situation and considering how we could have handled something differently or improved our performance. But sometimes, we don't take the time to reflect or we choose not to reflect, maybe because we don't want to consider the reality of the situation. This stops us from learning and improving, potentially causing us to repeat the same mistakes.

Supported reflection

Reflection is a powerful tool when developing and learning new ideas or concepts, either within a structured learning environment or within the workplace where a new way of thinking and working is being embraced. Reflection is where you take time to consider and review an experience; what you have taken away from it; how it will influence future ideas, decisions, or experiences; and what, if anything, you will change as a result.

Reflection is a cyclical process that usually consists of the following elements:

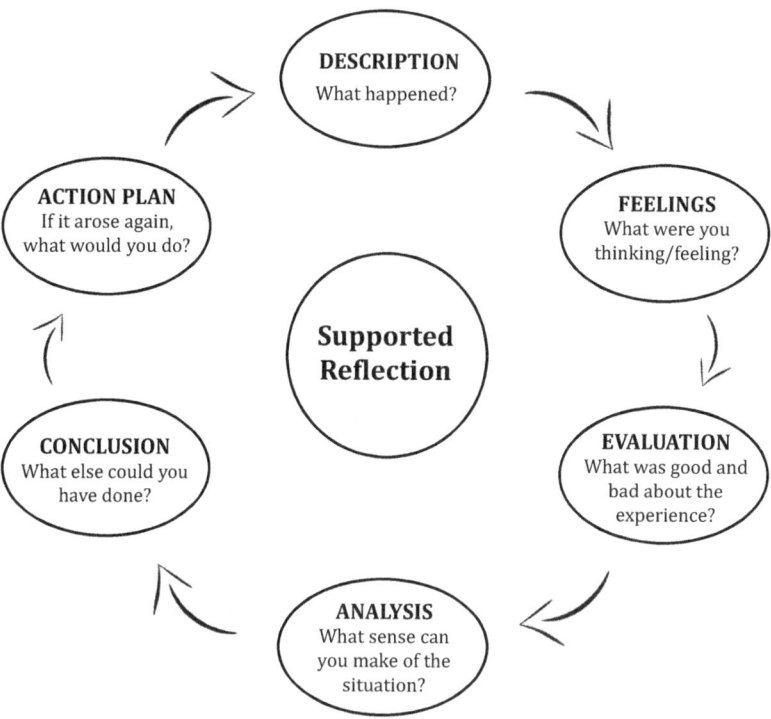

Far too many organisations provide learning and training without really considering the reflection element needed. All too often, we see a need as managers for staff to learn something and so we seek out a course or other suitable learning solution. Instead it may be possible for you to provide a learning experience by enabling the staff member to be involved in an activity, and then support them in reflecting on it to learn and develop through action.

> **Consider this...**
>
> In order to be more agile and able to respond to changing needs, it's necessary to ensure there is structure to the learning within your organisation. It's very easy for learning to become a knee-jerk reaction, for example, we have a change in need so we send some staff on a course to learn about the change, or we have a problem so we find a course or event to learn how to fix the problem. Start looking at ways that you can fill learning gaps so you are more able to respond and keep abreast of the changing marketplace. Consider how you can drive growth by maximising the talent you already have within your organisation, rather than looking externally for it.
>
> You need to know which areas you are weak in as an organisation so you know which areas you need to concentrate on. This will help you develop a stronger team. However, do not get distracted by developing skills that are not in line with your plans. You may benefit from creating a skills chart if you don't have one already. This helps you identify the skills you need now and those you are likely to need in the future and when. Then you can map who has those skills already within your organisation. Any gaps can be plugged as you start to approach the need for them.

Embrace your learning organisation

Learning across departments often enables new ideas to be developed and implemented as everybody involved understands each other's roles both day-to-day and within discreet projects. In addition, by working across departments, everyone can access expertise and subject-specific knowledge during all stages of developing an idea, using each other's abilities to complement one another, and thus making a more complete solution.

As a result of sharing knowledge and experiences, learning organisations are often more agile. This is because they are more aware of the skills they have within their workforce, who works well on specific tasks and in specific teams, so they can quickly and easily react to changes by putting the right project team together. By encouraging a more collaborative approach to learning, your teams can also be more agile. By sharing their learning together, they will become more aware of each other's abilities and know who to speak to when problems arise.

In short, a learning organisation is one that is continually learning and encourages learning among its people. It promotes the exchange of information between employees, and so creates a more knowledgeable workforce. This produces a very flexible organisation where people accept and adapt to new ideas and change through a shared vision, and encourage enterprising activities.

Developing stretchy staff

Sharing learning experiences with each other in a non-judgmental way so that everyone can benefit from each person's individual experiences need not be overcomplicated. This is something that can be done in team and department meetings and then disseminated in management and board meetings. In a learning organisation, learning logs can also be used as part of the structure in addition to mentoring, coaching, and learning sets or groups.

To develop a learning organisation, you need leadership skills to ensure that ideas are embraced and developed, and where suitable, pushed forward into the wider organisation. If you want to support an enterprising way of working, implementing the concept of a learning organisation is hugely beneficial.

In essence, as a leader, your role is to encourage the right type of learning and reflection to help your team progress. As staff members see that with effort and support they have moved forward and are capable of things they previously felt incapable of, they will naturally develop a growth mind-set. People with a growth mind-set possess the kind of perseverance and resilience needed to achieve creative solutions.

However, staff who are not supported but try something new and fail will have their closed mind-set ideas reinforced and will not see that they are able to try something new in the future.

Summary

Having a learning organisation is a vital part of creating an enterprising organisation. Learning can be seen as the rungs of a ladder, where each step on the ladder takes you nearer to growth. To enable your organisation to become a learning organisation:

- Learning needs to be company-wide and inclusive, and include reflection.
- An acceptance that failure is a part of learning ensures that people immerse themselves in enterprise.
- A mind-set for growth encourages learning and enterprise.

Chapter 8 –

Generating and Developing Enterprise Ideas

"Whilst enterprise is all in the idea development, don't think that it only takes a good idea to be successful" - **Developing ideas is fun, testing their robustness is about hard work.**

Developing a great idea is often seen as the biggest obstacle to being enterprising. But in fact, there are ideas all around you, and both you and your staff can come up with multiple ideas. Once you begin to spot opportunities and know what you're trying to achieve for your organisation, you will find it much easier.

Every problem or opportunity can have many solutions or ideas—and it is your staff who can help you identify the way forward due to their varied experiences and day-to-day dealings with your customers. In the past, it was common to lock senior staff away to brainstorm ideas, but that rarely provides the diverse ideas that your staff can generate when actively faced with a problem.

In this chapter, we will look at:

- How ideas are generated and who generates them

- Developing and rejecting ideas
- Moving ideas forward

Enterprising ideas can and do come from just about anywhere. In the past, ideas tended to come from senior staff, then the staff were asked to implement the idea. But this doesn't always work. Senior staff members can be out of touch or not in the best position to think of solutions and spot opportunities. By working with your staff members, you can help them to develop ideas that might then be spread out across the organisation.

Ideas do not need to be hugely innovative or dramatic — sometimes the smallest or basic of ideas can make a huge difference to an organisation. Indeed, a simple or ordinary idea that your team are keen to implement is better than a superior idea no one is inspired to take action on.

Enterprising ideas

Most enterprising ideas resolve a problem for someone. In addition, it is best if they can enable your organisation to achieve one of the following:

- **Save money** – For example, a restaurant chain could find a ways to save money by improving wastage and not over-ordering perishable items.

- **Improve or increase profitability** – The restaurant could start providing an earlier sitting for families to improve profits from the same number of tables and restaurant size.

- **Develop new ideas** - The restaurant could adapt their menus to offer allergen-free options.

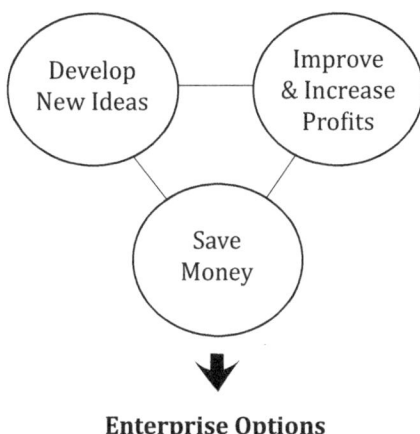

Enterprise Options

Whilst developing ideas, it's worth considering the three key areas of enterprise. It's possible to develop ideas in all three areas or just concentrate on one area.

Generating Ideas

For many people, actually generating an idea is the easy part, while for others, it seems like the worst thing in the world. Your team need to understand that initially, you are just coming up with ideas, so they don't need to be fantastic or hugely profitable at this stage. Nevertheless, it's worth looking at how different ideas can be generated.

How to generate ideas

Coming up with an idea requires time, and staff who don't have the time to think and allow their mind to wander are unlikely to come up with ideas. That's why we often hear people say they come up with great ideas in the shower or while out walking or driving. Their mind has been allowed the freedom to wander and consider random opportunities. This is hard to do when you're under pressure or are so busy with your daily tasks that your brain never has any downtime.

Some team members are naturally idea generators. For those who are not, or where you want whole teams to become more involved in enterprise, idea generation can be a fun place to start. Here are some ways you and your staff can come up with ideas:

- Learn more about the area you work in, new developments, and opportunities. By reading and learning more, it can open up new avenues and help spark an idea.

- Review the work of your direct and indirect competitors. By learning what others are doing, it can trigger an idea or help you spot a gap in the market.

- Speak to staff in different departments about things that are new or emerging within their field. New technologies and emerging markets can often help create a new idea.

- Network with people inside and outside your sector, and both your usual and non-usual client groups. Learn about their current difficulties and plans for the future to see whether you can create an idea that will help them.

- Get out and about in your local area, towns, and cities. Looking at any type of business can help trigger ideas. Review what's good and not so good about the way other businesses deliver services and sell products, and consider what you have learned. Is there anything you could take back to your organisation?

- Try being creative. Many people find that by doing something creative such as painting, their brain begins to wander and the creativity sparks new ideas.

- Exercise and a change of scenery can help you come up with new ideas. Many people advocate exercise, going for a walk or a run, or just getting out and about. Some even say that taking a bath or shower works for them. Much of it is about allowing your mind to drift.
- Run problem-solving sessions where people from different areas of the organisation come together to play about with ideas and try to solve problems.
- Look out for events on idea generation and enterprise, as these can help staff trigger ideas and make great connections with others attempting to be enterprising.
- Connect to others developing Enterprise Within™ in their organisation through social media groups on platforms such as LinkedIn.

There is no right or wrong way to come up with ideas. Some people find that connecting with their creative side or taking part in exercise helps, while others find a more structured review of current developments, technology, or industry leaders better. Whichever option works for you in coming up with new ideas—remember it is just the beginning. Don't get too swept up in the idea and romancing how it will look and how successful it might be before you've done more work on developing the idea and checking out its suitability.

Once ideas begin to flow, make sure you write them down, even those vague ideas and random thoughts. Let your mind and ideas drift and become more random—don't judge ideas as you come up with them—just write them down. Often, one idea will trigger another and another.

Who generates the ideas in organisational enterprise?

In reality, everyone has the potential to generate an idea.

However, some people seem more able to come up with ideas and solutions than others. This doesn't mean they are more enterprising, or even that they want to be involved in developing the ideas. Often, managers and leaders believe that staff who are good at innovation and idea generation are enterprising and staff who struggle to be innovative and come up with ideas are not. But this is not necessarily true. Idea generation is only one element of enterprise.

This is why it's worth running enterprise projects as teams, because each person can bring their individual strengths. Some people will be great at innovation and idea generation. For others, their skills are in developing the idea and making it work, or in motivating others to get involved and being proactive in implementing the idea.

Knowing that not everyone is good at idea generation helps to verify why idea generation should not be left to an individual or a small team, for example, of executives. Instead, it should be something that anyone at any level in the organisation can be involved in if they are able.

Should you work with others to develop your idea?

Sometimes, your idea may not be the best available. But if no one else knows you are working on it, they probably won't know that it's worth sharing their idea with you. There may be other ideas floating around in the organisation and by joining up ideas, you may develop an even better solution together. This means you must have the confidence to share your ideas with others and invite others to input into your idea.

Ideas generate ideas

Have you ever played the game on leadership training courses where you give groups of people some paperclips and ask each group to come up with ideas on what you can do with them? Often, in a matter of minutes, they come up with a range of ideas you may never have considered. In addition, the more they come up with ideas, the more they bounce off each other and generate more and more ideas. Many of these ideas may seem a little off-the-wall, but in general—ideas spark more ideas.

Supporting your staff to create suitable ideas is key to developing more ideas moving forward. Indeed, you may start with simple ideas and then gradually move on to bigger and more complex ideas. Running similar activities on sharing ideas can really spark some interesting new ideas.

Innovation or evolving an existing idea

Innovation and developing new ideas is often confused with coming up with a new product or new market idea that will cause a dramatic shift in the organisation. Whilst completely shifting the status quo is fantastic, it isn't necessary or indeed realistic for many organisations. Ideas can be about small shifts, changes to the way you deliver services, or improvements to products. Any change that helps an organisation be more successful and sustainable for the future is beneficial and shouldn't be disregarded just because it isn't a dramatic change.

To be enterprising, you need to develop various ideas from different options, then test them, try them, and drop those that don't work. Here are some options worth considering when looking at your ideas.

Is your idea about improvement? Do you already do something or make something that needs some improvements to make it more profitable, more sellable, or fit for the future? For example, if you're a car insurance company, do you lose customers due to poor customer service? After looking at other service providers such as banks, do you have ideas on how you can provide a better telephone service?

Is your idea opportunistic? Have you just spotted an opportunity and decided to go with it—even if it isn't really in your area of experience or expertise? Each type of idea has its pros and cons—you just need to decide which one suits your organisation and abilities. As a car insurance company, have you realised that many of your customers own a car and a motorbike but only use one at a time? If so, can you offer a package option for them?

Is your idea building upon previous ideas? Once you have an initial idea, are you building on it by adding more and more detail, options, or scope? For example, if the initial business idea was selling car insurance, are you now looking at how you can offer other services to the same audience, such as other insurance products or other services linked to their car?

Is your idea about being a specialist? Are you trying to become known as the experts in your field? Growing your business by being known as the best or the only one in your specific area can be a viable focus. For example, rather than just selling car insurance, could you just sell car insurance for prestige or vintage car owners?

Is your idea innovative? Are you developing something new or offering it in a new way? Could you offer a new type of car insurance for a particular client group who no one currently serves?

Is your idea adding to the evolutionary funnel? Are you taking something that already exists but updating it or moving the idea forward, such as utilising new technology to improve something? Could you use technology to offer pay-as-you-drive car insurance?

Is your idea about saving money? Often, enterprising solutions are born from necessity, such as the need to save money. This means doing something differently and in a more cost-effective way, making purchasing changes, etc. Can you change the way you process payments, sell services, or carry out administrative tasks in order to reduce the overall costs to the organisation?

Is your idea about doing more of the same? It's possible that your idea is to keep doing what you are already doing because you are good at it, but to spread your audience and reach a wider customer net. Have you spotted ways you could capture more customers by offering a wider range of products or breaking into a new market or country?

Is your idea about adding value to your current offerings? There are many ways we can add value by offering different levels of service, more specialist elements, or extra options. Do you have connections with another organisation, such as a breakdown company, so you can offer a bundle option of car insurance and breakdown cover to entice new customers?

Is your idea about something completely new? New products or services can be added as complementary products or easy add-ons to your current work. As well as offering car insurance, could you also offer car loans?

Importantly, remember that the most successful enterprising ideas are born from a need that someone has. Your enterprise project should be about solving that need. If you are offering them something you already know people need rather than chasing what you think they want, you've already won half the battle to having a successful enterprise.

Helping your team come up with ideas

Ideas can come from anywhere, so it's important not to feel that ideas must be tried and tested, or even that your team need to develop something unusual or different. The ideas you consider and work on need to suit you and your organisation's needs and abilities.

Whilst for some, the concept of developing a new idea may seem like a fun and exciting prospect, for other people it will be daunting. Many people worry that they may not have any ideas, or only ideas that are unsuitable. Others worry they may develop ideas that are later rejected, or that their idea may be implemented and not work. I've even seen people unable to stick to an idea out of fear that there is a better idea out there. Whilst any idea from you or your team needs to be carefully considered in order to become a successful project, it doesn't have to be fully formed from the start.

Ideas shouldn't be dismissed too early on, as often with some thought and development, they can become much stronger than the initial concept. Your role is to help everyone share their ideas and then work through the ideas, improving them and potentially adding two different ideas together to form a better solution. Take the stance that no idea is a bad idea and they should all be considered. This way, staff will feel more willing to tell you about random ideas that may seem no good at face value, but often with some refinement, can be ideal.

Developing stretchy staff

In order to come up with new ideas, we need to be open to seeing new things and trying new ways of doing things. The best way to do this is for staff to get out and about, considering how others do things and whether they could implement similar ideas. Encourage your staff to stretch their imaginations and stretch their minds when they are away from the workplace.

Enterprise Within™

Selling your idea to others

Once a member of staff or a team decides that they have an idea or would like to work on something enterprising, they will need to get buy-in from you, as their manager or leader. In turn, you may need to justify the idea to a more senior team or board.

Before you can sell an idea, you need to be realistic about it, as other people will be able to identify the pros and the cons for themselves. This means you need to be prepared — accept that they may see only the risks, and be armed with responses explaining how you will mitigate the risks, overcome obstacles, and manage difficulties. Also, don't forget to research the benefits — provide them with real-life examples, facts and figures, and case studies to help them make a decision in your favour.

If you are supporting a member of your team in pitching their idea, you can help them by arming them with this knowledge, working through any possible objections with them, as well as guiding them to provide a solid business case.

Either you or your team need to be able to present the idea in a professional way and understand things from a decision-maker's points of view. You may be asking your manager to consider things they have previously dismissed or are fearful of. But remember that with great risk comes great rewards. Any decision-maker will want to know why you think your idea is a good idea. Have examples of similar ideas, either in your own organisation or other businesses. They will value you presenting some sort of business case on the viability and benefits of taking the idea forward.

When ideas aren't suitable

If someone's ideas are dismissed, be aware that this individual can quickly become a disruptor in your team.

They may become difficult to manage as they start to feel less and less appreciated and their abilities under-valued. This often results in them leaving. Staff who have ideas need to be managed correctly to ensure they don't become disruptors.

If you encourage people to develop ideas, it's important to consider how you will either implement their ideas or reject them with an explanation. You need to explain to staff members why an idea is or isn't being used, or if it is being altered. If not, they will feel that their work and effort is not worthwhile or valued by their employers. By encouraging them to come up with and work on their ideas, they are likely to become more engaged in their work and more committed and engaged with their employer.

Be ready for managers to refuse your idea if it's too similar to one that has previously failed. Accept that you may need to go away and do more development or research, and if they reject your first option, don't forget to ask for a second opportunity to present a rework of your idea later.

Moving your ideas forward

It's important to review all ideas. This can be done by asking staff to submit ideas on a standard idea form or give a presentation. The most important thing is to ensure that staff know how ideas can be submitted, who will be reviewing them, and when.

When you feel you have selected one or two key ideas, you will be keen to start developing the ideas for your enterprise. You will need to understand how and why your team should be involved. From here, you are entering into the development and implementation phase of your idea, turning it into a real enterprise project. This requires structure as it becomes a project in its own right. But for now, your role is to champion the idea and make sure it's moved forward into project implementation.

This may require you to keep on top of what's happening with the idea, who is going to be project managing it, and when it will be actioned. As a leader, you may need to keep nudging people to ensure the idea becomes a reality.

When an idea fails

Ideas can and do fail. This is all part of enterprise. Remember, the key is to use failure as a learning tool. If you are testing your ideas before implementing them, failure should occur before there are any major implications. However, at any stage when things don't work out, you need to be ready to take it in your stride. Consider the following elements to make sure you deal with failure in the best way possible:

- Make sure you review and reflect so that you can understand what went wrong and how to avoid it next time.

- Avoid blame. It's easy to lay blame on an individual, team, or circumstances, but this can affect future projects and ideas from being successful. Who will fancy working on future ideas if they know they will be blamed for failures?

- Take the time to learn from failures and see what you can take forward for future plans.

- Give staff time to accept and come to terms with the failure. But *do* look at new ideas because one failure doesn't mean you can't do it. It just means you need to do something different.

Sometimes, ideas fail because of the timing, resources, or willingness of the team to take an idea on board. Whatever the reason for your idea failing, your role is to ensure that staff don't become unwilling to try new ideas in the future.

Developing your ideas

When an organisation decides to implement new ideas, it usually starts by developing, researching, and preparing, then rolling it out. If it doesn't work when it's rolled out, it's stopped and deemed a failure. This is a huge waste of time and money, and means a whole new idea has to be considered and moved through the same process of development.

Speeding up the idea implementation process can be the difference between getting to a marketplace first or missing out on a new opportunity because you are too slow to progress an idea. To do this, test labs are becoming popular within organisations as a way of working through multiple ideas and developing them simultaneously before selecting the right ones to roll out, which we'll look at shortly.

Whatever change, idea, or enterprise project you decide to implement, you will no doubt do your research, spend time developing the idea, designing how it will work, and discussing it with all interested parties. After lots of planning meetings, you will implement the idea. If it's a change that affects the whole organisation, you may even implement it throughout the organisation. Then—and only then—will you find out whether it actually works, and whether people will commit to the new idea.

Now you're probably wondering what happens if it doesn't work? Or if it does, but not completely or not how you meant it to? Yikes! This can happen, of course. Whilst there is no definite way of making sure your idea is perfect before you roll it out completely, it may be worth considering testing your ideas out before they go completely live.

There are various ways of testing ideas, such as sampling a product or service on a small group of current or potential customers, getting your internal customers (staff) to try out ideas, piloting ideas with discreet groups of people willing to give you feedback, or using test labs.

What are test labs?

Test labs or project test labs are often used to enable employees to try out new ideas. They offer the ability to test, review, and re-test before you finally implement your idea. Test labs may sound like a medical research building, but in fact, they don't have to be anything physical at all. Test labs are a process that can be developed to suit your organisation's needs.

On the whole, test labs provide a safe place to develop an idea, grow the idea, and roll it out with a safe group of people to see whether it works. There is then the opportunity to review and reflect on how it went and what needs altering before you either test it again or roll it out on a larger scale. This gives staff members the opportunity to test their ideas and work on them before rolling them out company-wide. In addition, test labs often give staff members time away from their usual workload and access to people who can support them. For some people, in order to be enterprising and think creatively, they need time and space — and a test lab can do just that.

If you are a large organisation with multiple enterprise ideas being tested at any one time, you may have some office space set aside for people to work in. You may allow staff to work collaboratively, have access to specialists within the office, and use the tools they need to easily test ideas without having to hunt around or keep asking for things. Yet for a smaller organisation, it may just be a simple system or process that staff can access and follow to try out their ideas.

By running new ideas as tests or pilots, it's possible to test more than one idea at a time. For example, you may have multiple staff members or groups working on similar ideas at the same time and seeing which provides the best solution. This enables you to roll out only those likely to be successful, holding back or curtailing the development of other ideas. This can speed up the improvement process, rather than trying one idea at a time until the right solution is found.

This method of experimental testing is becoming more prevalent in large organisations that wish to speed up change by checking out ideas and ensuring they will work before implementing them. It helps ensure that all parameters are clear before suggesting that everyone in the organisation adopts something new. It also provides an opportunity for different departments to test and adapt an idea until the best solution is developed.

Most organisations put a timeframe and budget restrictions in place when testing ideas. Many keep test lab projects under tight review and scrutiny. These are not play things. This is about serious development and the implementation of new and beneficial ideas. On the whole, try to speed up the creation of ideas through the process of development, not only because new ideas are often time-critical, but also because it's important not to spend too much time on ideas that are not likely to work.

Dealing with risk through testing

Much of enterprise is about testing and trying ideas, then developing the right solutions based on evidence. When we come up with new ideas, new ways of doing things, or different solutions, there is always an element of risk. However, by testing, you can lower the risk – giving various formats and solutions a go before fully adopting the one that best suits the organisation, team, customers, and management.

Regular and supportive feedback is necessary to keep an idea on track. However you design it, your test lab requires supportive staff who have the skills to develop the ideas and give honest feedback to ensure it is developed to provide the best outcome possible.

Enterprise Within™

Using test labs to enhance an idea

Test labs can be used not only to take an idea, develop it into a project, and then turn into a real-life working solution, but also to help take a rough idea and develop it into a more complete idea moving forward.

Some companies have taken test labs to the next level and developed corporate enterprise accelerator models. These provide a physical space, finance, and all the other R&D tools and technologies needed in one place. Staff are often moved to work exclusively within this accelerator program.

In a test lab situation, it allows staff to work on an idea outside their usual working environment. This different environment can, in its own right, help with the innovation of the idea. In addition, being surrounded by other people who are also working on innovative ideas leads to discussions and conversations, and these can generate and spark further ideas. By removing distractions, it's possible to work on ideas in a concentrated way and develop them into the next phase. So, provide opportunities for people to come together physically or virtually to suit your working environment.

Experimenting with different approaches is worth considering. It can be easy to fall into the trap of trying something, accepting it works, and sticking with that idea without considering the other options. Experimenting in a structured and considered way enables an individual to see whether any other methods would be better, or whether the first idea worked and should be rolled out.

Side-by-side testing of similar ideas to decide the best option can also be a valuable option. Either similar options can be developed simultaneously so you can select the option most likely to succeed, or you can use the two ideas to develop and learn from each other.

Whichever testing option you choose, it will ensure that you only go for the full-scale introduction of an idea after you have tried it and validated its value and potential success. Some organisations choose to test product ideas on their own staff before testing on real clients, and then only in a phased approach. In essence, how you test is up to you, but never test alone without feedback and support from others, as it can be easy to believe that something is really great or really rubbish instead of seeing the reality. Only with support and feedback can you get a better perspective.

Support and review through test labs

Enterprise activities require a format to ensure you are continuously reviewing and reflecting on the idea and how it's progressing. Without such an approach, the activities can often loose traction or direction. Test labs are able to offer such support in a cohesive way.

Within your test lab structure, you can build in opportunities for individuals with specific expertise to work alongside staff as they develop their ideas. By having people with specific expertise in various elements, they can provide feedback and encourage reflection and reviews as they go along.

You could also look to have one overall person to act as a mentor, guide, and motivator. This person can not only provide support, but also a formal reflection and review of the work as it progresses in a holistic way rather than focusing on specific aspects. They can often also provide connections and links to the right people and help with any challenges along the way.

Leading innovative staff as they develop ideas

You must decide how you will lead and support your staff

members as they develop and work on enterprising ideas and projects. It is possible to have different solutions for different projects. Some projects may require significant time and commitment to bring them to fruition, while others may be easy to develop and adopt across the organisation with just some simple alterations.

Some employers choose to provide staff with set days / times of the week or month to work on new ideas, while others may choose to release all staff from their usual duties to concentrate completely on their new idea. You may feel it's worth setting time limits. For example, some employers only allow staff short periods of time in the test lab environment, either combining this work with their usual duties in an acceptable time split or constraining their time to a certain number of weeks on developing the idea.

If the idea is still not ready in that time, then it is reviewed and reconsidered to see who is best to look into it further, if indeed it's worth any further development at all. By having limits, it will avoid staff from becoming too disconnected with their day-to-day work.

Summary

A big part of enterprise is developing the ideas that will take the organisation forward. When generating and developing ideas, keep the following points in mind:

- Enterprise ideas can be about resolving a problem, saving money, increasing profits, or developing new ideas.
- Ideas don't have to be unusual, big, or complex — they can be simple or small.
- Give your staff time to come up with ideas and support them in creating ideas.

- Run enterprise projects as teams to benefit from different team members' skills.
- Consider and work through every idea even if it seems unlikely at first. Improve the ideas and potentially combine them to form a better solution.
- Review ideas and always feed back to staff whether they are taken forward or not.
- Minimise risk by implementing test labs to try out ideas before committing to rolling them out and regularly review your progress.
- When ideas fail, use them as tools for learning to improve in the future.
- Have a mentor or person in place to support individuals through the development process.

Chapter 9 -

Developing an Enterprise Project – It's All in the Planning

"Build a stronger business through planned enterprise projects."

Developing an enterprise project and ensuring it has every chance of success requires structure and certain areas to be considered. It's easiest to think of an enterprise project as a mini-business, and therefore it needs a mini-business plan.

This plan will clarify your enterprise idea, how it will be developed, implemented, and rolled out. Planning the development of a new enterprise should be a team effort and make use of everyone's ideas, knowledge, and experience to enable your idea to be as successful as possible. The clearer the plan, the easier it is for everyone involved to know the part they play in the development of the project.

In this chapter, we will look at:

- How to develop an enterprise project plan—what to consider.
- The process needed to actually develop the enterprise idea.

The 8-step enterprise project process

Once you have identified the right idea and the right staff, it's important to ensure that the idea is given every chance to succeed. The best way to do this is to develop the idea into an enterprise project. No two enterprise projects are the same and no two journeys on the enterprise route are exactly the same either. However, there is a process that will help ensure your enterprise project is successful. Having an overall plan will help everyone keep on track, and will also enable you to identify your overall vision for the idea or enterprise project.

The overall process will ensure you know the short-term and long-term aims for the project and the route you are taking to achieve them. The following process is easy to follow and will help keep your enterprise project on track.

Enterprise Within™

 # Creating Your Enterprise Project

1
- Generate as many ideas as possible working alone, in teams, with stakeholders, and with customers.
- Review each idea, considering how suitable it is for your organisation, abilities, skills, costs, etc.

2
- Select which idea to work on by considering the profitability, likely success, or ability to get started.
- Check you have buy-in from your team and other important people such as the senior team, executives, stakeholders, and clients.

3
- Develop plans, drawings, prototypes, or samples of your products and services.
- Develop and write up action plans, business plans, and marketing plans to help develop the idea further.

4
- Is it possible to test run your idea? Roll-out prototypes etc? Look for a sample group to test.
- Evaluate the test run and develop roll-out plans.

5
- Resources are precious, so consider what resources you will need to take your idea to the next level.

6
- Pitch the roll-out plan to the executive team / board and then those who will be involved in rolling it out.
- Pitch the idea to investors / funders.

7
- Check your plans and launch the idea.
- Review your plans and evaluate during and after launch.

8
- Review the success of the idea.
- Develop new ideas.
- Keep growing the ideas and organisation.

We'll now look at the considerations at each stage in detail.

1. Generate

Generate your initial ideas using the ideas from previous chapters. Keep in mind that an enterprising project is likely to be one of three formats:

- A project that **saves money** by making a change that may also improve services or reduce time and costs.

- A project that takes what you already do and **adds value**, such as upselling to another client or client group, re-purposing or re-packaging the offering to suit a different client group, or adding something in order to charge higher rates / increase profits.

- A **new idea / project** that will provide a different offering, potentially to the same or a different audience. This is a larger-scale project that is likely one day to spin out as a social enterprise in its own right.

On the whole, ideas work when they are based on marketplace need, so you need to consider: do you have a possible customer base that is going to buy at a level that will be profitable for you? Has anyone else been successful with this idea and has anyone else tried and failed? If so, why did they fail and how will you overcome these potential barriers?

2. Select

If you have several ideas or versions of an idea, it is worth gaining input from anyone who will become involved in the project. By involving others in selecting the idea, they are more likely to feel involved and committed, plus they may be able to give their opinion on the options based on previous experiences.

Clarify your reasoning for embarking on your enterprise journey. This is your **why**. When you understand why you are doing it or why it is important, this will ensure you select the right idea. Starting up a new enterprise project takes time and energy and will require any individuals involved to drive it forward, so the more everyone is sure *why* they are doing it and understand the reasoning behind the new enterprise, the more likely they are to put in the extra effort required.

Start considering questions such as:

- What do you want this new enterprise project to achieve? E.g. increased income, improved profits, larger client base, more opportunities to expand.

- How does your enterprise project sit with your organisation goals, values, and mission? E.g. will it distract you from your longer-term mission as an organisation? Does it add to your core goals around customer care? Will it enable you to meet more of your organisation values around staff involvement or community / charity support?

- What staff and management time can you free up to develop the idea? E.g. is there an endless supply of time or is it limited to a set number of hours, certain days, or specific staff members?

- What investment do you need to put into the enterprise project? E.g. does it need upfront investment or staged payments to support its development as the idea comes to fruition?

- What implications are there for the organisation when working on the new enterprise project? E.g. distraction from usual work, escalating costs for the new enterprise project?

Remember, just because you select one idea to work on, it doesn't mean any other ideas have been completely rejected.

You may come back to those ideas later depending on the success, or not, of the first option.

Keep in mind that when individuals have come up with an idea, they may be concerned if it is selected to be moved forward. Reassure them that no one individual is solely responsible for the potential success or failure of the idea. The more this is done within an organisation, the more other staff will become involved in enterprise projects, as they will not feel anxious about sharing their ideas and views.

3. Develop

Following on from this, it's likely that the idea will need even more development to ensure it's suitable to move forward. At this point, stretch your thinking to see other opportunities, do your research around areas such as potential marketplace and customers, and assess the ability, skills, and time of your staff to move the idea forward.

By considering other options and possible solutions, as you develop the idea you can ensure that all areas are properly considered. The aim here is to develop an idea in a way that avoids blunders and costly oversights as much as possible. Make sure that the ideas are not overcomplicated, as this can lead to increases in complexity of the enterprise project and costs.

Resources and structure

One of your biggest resources is likely to be your team, as they are the ones who will enable this project to go ahead. How much time do they really have available to put into a new idea? You may decide it's best to set limits on the amount of time staff members can work on the project, and when they can work on it. Be realistic about how much time it will need and how much you can afford to invest.

The cost of other materials and resources need to be considered at all stages. Consider the cost implications of both the failure and success of the project. Mistakes are an inevitable part of developing new enterprise projects, however, the costs do need to be considered and you may need to set budgets and limit spending. Continually review how much time and money a project has cost, and how close it is to being rolled out. Clearly, the higher the potential return if the idea is successful, the more you may be willing to invest in an idea without knowing that it will work.

4. Test

During the testing phase, make sure you use all the skills and knowledge you have available within the organization to give this idea the best opportunity of success. Far too often, organisations launch ideas without speaking to people who could have helped them make it even better. The easiest way to ensure you have the right people supporting your enterprise project is to invite key people from different functions within your organisation to be involved in a project meeting, where the idea is discussed from its reasons to its aims.

Give others the opportunity to share their experiences and input into the idea to help develop it further. In addition, they can offer their expertise, time, and practical support during the testing phase. For example, if your IT team is working on a better online tool for customer orders, then key staff members from the sales team, customer services, and even the production team can help ensure the best solution is developed and tested.

Bring in advisors and supporters you completely trust to tell you the truth. They can often see things that need changing — not because they are better than the team who is involved, but because they are not as emotionally invested in the idea or as close to it.

5. Pitch

Once an idea has been tested, you will probably need to pitch it to the senior executive team for their approval to roll it out further or launch the enterprise idea as a new product or service. Some of the things you will need to cover in your pitch include:

- Have you considered how much support is needed both from the internal team and any external expertise?
- What will you need to move the enterprise idea forward in terms of materials, facilities, or input from others?
- Can you begin to indicate the potential income, profits, or other benefits that developing the idea will bring to the organisation?

6. Launch

This is often the most exciting, but equally the most disconcerting point, in the enterprise project. Launching a new idea is likely to need the support of marketing, PR, and other experts. From the perspective of the team behind the projects, this is when all their efforts will be judged as successful or not. Your role as the leader is to offer them support and encouragement in these final stages of the development work and help them move forward into the roll-out phase. Don't be shocked if self-doubt creeps in here with your team as they realise that their new idea is about to be seen and potentially judged by others for the first time.

It's worth considering how you will celebrate this landmark point with the team, though they also need to be aware of the need to continually drive and deliver. All too often, organisations forget to allow staff time to celebrate the success of launching a great idea. Don't fall into this trap.

7. Grow

When the idea has been launched, it's not time to sit back. You need to continue to grow the idea and move it forward — continually improving it and finding ways of growing your organisation. Consider looking at:

- Ways to add to the current idea and use it to develop further.
- Ideas that will sit closely with the current project and help it grow.
- Ideas that enable you to utilise the new skills developed by the team in the original idea.

8. Review

Having a plan is great, but as always, spending time reviewing and reflecting on the plan is vital. Knowing whether this plan will work in the future will enable you and your team to move future ideas forward even quicker. They will know the process and format of taking an idea from generation through to launch, and this will help them in the future when they are considering bringing a new idea forward.

Summary

When you have developed some potential enterprising ideas, you need to turn them into reality. The best way to do this is create enterprise projects.

- Turn ideas into enterprise projects to ensure their success.
- Follow the simple 8-step process laid out in this chapter to develop an enterprise project.
- Ensure you consider the important points at each stage.

Chapter 10 –

Supporting and Managing Enterprising Staff

"Entrepreneurs do it alone – enterprising organisations do it collaboratively."

As a leader, you need to help your staff members by removing as many barriers as possible to enable them to be enterprising. Your role is to encourage enterprise in all staff, give additional support to them, and identify those who have the potential to implement new ideas and be the change-makers in your organisation. When you have inspired your teams to be enterprising, you need to continue to encourage and enable enterprising activities. In supporting such activities, you can help your organisation grow.

In this chapter, you will:

- Find out how to support and manage your staff as the leader
- Know what type of relationships you need with your staff
- Discover what to do when staff make mistakes
- See why reflection is vital
- Consider how to reward your staff

Your role as the leader is to provide your staff with support and encouragement so they can implement and take advantage of suitable options, opportunities, and ideas. It will provide them with a guiding hand so they feel able to take action that can add value to the organisation.

Enterprising staff: what you need to know as a manager

Staff who are more willing to be involved in enterprising projects tend to have certain traits and working styles. They can adapt themselves and are more willing to work outside the core requirements of their role. This difference in style will need a different type of support from managers and leaders.

If you think back to the traits of an enterprising person discussed in chapter one, it included being a self-starter or a self-motivated person. These staff members are often people who are willing to get on with things. They don't feel the need to check with others that they can work on their own initiative.

Whilst it's great to have staff who are enthusiastic and driven in this way, it may require some elements of your usual management style to be modified. Part of your role is to ensure your staff members are adding value to the organisation with their activities.

In this, a balance is required. Whilst you wish to encourage individuals to push forward, make changes, and implement new ideas, they must also be aware of the bigger picture, and the organisation's needs and structures. As the leader, you need to ensure that the bigger picture is both understood and considered at all points of an enterprise project.

Some enterprise activities can cause friction with other staff members and you will need to guide them so this can be alleviated. You will need to guide them and keep them on track. Don't expect them to keep you fully informed or check in with you before doing something. Be ready for this and help them to keep the project running smoothly without causing any great problems.

You definitely don't want to quash the entrepreneurial spirit in staff members. However, you do need to remember that while some staff members may embrace this new enterprising vibe, others will not be so keen. This may require some careful handling of team members and mediation skills on occasions.

You need to remember that for many, the idea of developing an enterprise project can be a big change from their traditional way of working. For many individuals, teams, and organisations, there will be a shift in culture and this can be unsettling.

Developing stretchy staff

A team is tasked to create an enterprise project to develop a new service for their estate agency. The idea is to offer house makeovers, cleaning, and odd job repairs to properties before or whilst they are on the market to help secure a sale. The clients can buy this additional service through the office and the team developing it are looking at rolling it out to a small selection of clients. However, the admin team in the office don't feel they are best placed to handle enquiries, as they don't understand the pricing structure or how to manage the work. In fact, they feel that the new project team are pushing them to agree to things before they are even ready to roll out.

To avoid friction, the manager needs to help the teams understand each other's perspectives. The administration team need to understand that the new project team are not being unreasonable – they are just excited about

> their project and anxious to make it successful. The enterprise team need to understand that the administration team are busy already and can only help if they fully understand what's required of them and know how to implement it correctly. For them, their relationships with the clients are key and they worry that if they are not fully informed, it will affect their client relationships.
>
> The manager needs to step in here and help both sides understand the difficulties and consider how to move the ideas forward. Staff need to stretch themselves and consider things from other people's points of view.

Developing a shared purpose

When we look at encouraging enterprise in the workplace, it's really about developing a shared understanding of the future, of what it will look like, and how the organisation can get there. This understanding enables staff to understand their purpose and role in enterprise projects.

If your staff don't know what is expected of them, how will they know how to keep an eye out for suitable ideas and opportunities? If they don't understand why you are aiming to be more enterprising, then they will struggle to buy into the idea or connect with the enterprising projects you are trying to implement.

The staff you have selected to work on enterprising projects probably already feel committed to helping the organisation grow. However, the staff who are not involved are likely to feel even more removed from the concept. Some may see it as threatening their future stability, some may feel it's a silly idea, and others may feel they should block such enterprising projects. I call these people "Enterprise Blockers".

Enterprise blockers

Some people will feel distrust or dislike the idea of these new enterprise projects for a variety of reasons. Whilst they may not be directly involved in the enterprise projects you have planned without them on board, they can still have a detrimental effect. They can influence the success or otherwise of any enterprising projects. They can affect projects through miscommunication, mismanagement, and general sabotage.

Enterprise enabler

As a leader, you must be an enterprise enabler, but it is also possible for staff who are not directly involved in enterprise projects to also be enterprise enablers. Their role is to support enterprise activities and add to the commercial nature of the organisation. For example, they can impact the view of stakeholders and the wider community of your organisation through their own actions. Whilst many may not realise that their actions are directly related to enterprise activities, they can often be damaging.

Case study

A college is trying to increase its commercial work with local employers. The team involved in these enterprising projects understand the need for good relationships, and they work hard to build these relationships with local employers and stakeholders.

However, other staff members in the college do not understand their impact on such relationships. Both current and past experiences of connecting with local employers has on the whole been negative and some teaching staff seem to be continually undermining the work of the enterprise team. These staff would be seen as enterprise blockers. Their behaviour is affecting the ability of others to carry out enterprise activities.

Internal competitiveness

Staff may feel the need to hold back information or keep ideas secret if they believe someone else may take the idea and develop it themselves. As the leader or manager, you need to ensure that this is removed from the equation as much as possible. Knowledge sharing and trust is core to innovation development and a more enterprising culture. You can easily provide staff with a structured way of sharing ideas so they can be tracked back to their originator. This will also mean staff can develop ideas through collaboration, build on initial ideas by working together, and improve the idea through shared experiences and knowledge.

The culture needs to be one of not just trust and willingness to take responsibility, but a shared purpose in developing the organisation. By enabling others to feel part of the organisation, its decision-making, and its growth, they will be more willing and able to provide support and be less focused on competing with others.

Encouraging enterprise

As the leader, you need to be encouraging enterprise in

others. Some of the best ways to support and encourage enterprise are around culture and focusing on how you want the organisation to move forward.

1) **Be inclusive.** Whilst entrepreneurship is often a lonely path to travel, enterprise within organisations shouldn't be. Successful enterprise projects in workplaces are often developed by a small group of people and supported by the wider team. By involving and encouraging the wider organisation to play its part, they can feel part of the journey. They will therefore support it and add value as and when applicable. This will also encourage others to be more enterprising and enable all staff members to feed into ideas. This will help staff to develop a greater understanding and knowledge of the idea's implementation.

2) **Shout about it.** One of the best ways of rewarding those involved in new projects is to shout about their work commitment and progress to the rest of the staff. Staff want to feel included and aware of new projects, just as much as those involved in the projects want others to know about their good work.

3) **Be as you want others to be.** The best way to get staff to think in a more enterprising way is to be, yes you guessed it, enterprising yourself. To show you are serious about it, develop goals and opportunities for staff to become creative and put things into place to enable innovation. Add it as a discussion point to team meetings, staff appraisals, and annual reviews.

4) **Enable innovation by being open to ideas.** This sounds so simple, but often staff who come up with ideas go to their managers or senior executives only to be told it's not what they want or it's not "thought through enough". Telling them to go away can put some off bothering next time.

5) **Set time aside.** Allow time in people's schedules to focus on new ideas and innovative solutions. When staff are constantly working at full speed on things, it's hard to see other options. Consider offering a block of time on a regular basis or more ad hoc options for staff to take time away and work on ideas.

6) **Avoid blame.** The quickest way to put staff off coming forward is if they believe that the company has a blame culture or a tendency not to support people when ideas don't work out or problems occur. It's inevitable with new things that there will be some teething problems, but individuals or teams should not be blamed. Instead, they should be supported and encouraged to work through the problems and find solutions.

7) **Don't be dull.** Many businesses are boring, slow, and reluctant to change. Enterprising people will often move on from this type of organisation and offer their skills to a more innovative company. This can lead to a spiral where you end up with the staff who don't have drive and ambition, and are unlikely to come up with innovative ideas. The organisation will become increasingly dull and will find it difficult to recruit in the right staff. To encourage innovation and creativeness, you will need to create a less boring place to be and work.

8) **Remove permission hierarchies.** Much of the lower-level enterprise activities are about reacting to a situation, in the moment, in an appropriate way. When staff work within a system where they must have permission to do something outside their standard activities, it will quash their ability and willingness to be innovative.

Supporting enterprise

As the leader, your role in supporting enterprise is often a combination of offering your hands-on support and knowledge, as well as using your experience to mentor other staff members to carry out enterprise projects. It can be easy to help with the development of an idea phase, but don't forget some of the others core areas such as:

- What is the enterprise project about? (The overall plan)
- Why are you committed to the project? (Your reasoning)
- What is the long-term goal for the project? (The end goal)
- How do you envisage the idea coming to fruition (The strategy)
- What resources does it need? (The finance)

Keep these elements in mind when you are supporting enterprise projects. One of the best options to support staff involved in enterprise is to offer mentoring support.

Enterprise mentoring

The role of the mentor in enterprise is about helping to develop business knowledge and connecting the individual/s to the right people. This will help them develop their skills and knowledge as well as their idea. Some of the things you may need to help staff learn about can include:

- Commerciality
- Business models
- Business finance

- Economics
- Developing good communication skills
- Tolerance for ambiguity
- Persistence
- Leadership
- Resolving conflict
- Cross-team effectiveness

Managing expectations

It's important to manage the expectations of your staff members. Whilst it can be beneficial to involve a staff member in developing their idea, it may not be possible or practical to do so. In these cases, the manager's role can be about helping the staff member to understand the value they have added — even if they are no longer involved. Keeping them informed and ensuring they get recognition for their idea can help.

Accountability, ownership of work, and fear of failure

Much of enterprise work is about becoming comfortable with the unknown. If staff are not sure what could happen, or there could be repercussions, unwanted additional work, or responsibility, they may avoid putting forward ideas or working on enterprising projects.

In order to encourage and support enterprise, it's necessary to adopt a more open approach to trying new ideas, accepting mistakes, seeing the need for change, and understanding alterations to plans. You also need to look at how you can improve staff members' ownership of work and accepting accountability.

A lack of accountability will suggest to staff that it's okay to lower their standards, take risks, and not worry about the consequences. This is obviously not acceptable. Whilst I never advocate a blame culture, accountability is necessary. Holding people accountable for poor decisions, bad quality work, poor attitudes, and unacceptable actions is necessary. Having those difficult conversations with teams and individuals will also be required at times.

First, find out the truth, learn about the situation, see what happened, and discover how it came about. Find out whether it is the team or particular individuals involved, then have a conversation with them about their actions. Ask them why they thought they should do what they did and how it went wrong. This alone may be enough. For many people, talking it through, seeing how they impacted on the situation, and knowing how it can be avoided in the future is enough for them to realise their part and avoid it the next time. Others may need help in identifying what went wrong, how it can be avoided, and how to move forward.

Always work with staff to help them understand the problem and how to move forward, but ensure they realise the part they played and how this can't be continually repeated. Most of all, follow up with your team, help them move forward, and offer support so no one feels that if things go wrong, they are held accountable.

When people take action without trusting in those around them, it's the result of them concluding that they may as well do so. Often, taking action out of frustration can be dangerous. When trust has gone, there is little left to lose.

Developing a more supportive and powerful work environment

As the leader, keep an eye out for enterprise blockers,

organisational bureaucracy, hierarchy, rules, and individuals that hinder the enterprising staff members. Your role is to support staff so they can overcome these enterprise blockers.

You can, as the leader, develop a positive attitude towards risk and experimentation. You need to work with your teams so that all ideas are discussed and any risks are known and considered. Then, by working closely throughout the enterprise project, and with regular feedback and support, you will be kept in touch with the progress and any impending risks. By embracing learning, helping teams to work together through problems, and keeping communication open and honest, risk can be reduced.

Set aside reflection time. This can take place individually in mentoring sessions and as a team in staff meetings. Reflection can be used to spot problems before they occur, reflect on problems in their early stages, understand why they have happened and how to fix them, and know how to avoid them in the future. In addition, reflection can help teams see new opportunities and possible new solutions. This reflection time needs to be built into the very essence of your organisation in order to see enterprising activities spread.

Your role is to develop relationships based on trust, dependability, and open communication—so you and your team can work in a safe environment to develop the best solutions possible.

Understanding the lifecycle of enterprise

One thing that can really help staff members understand how to implement ideas and develop enterprising solutions is to understand the lifecycle of enterprise. This can help them understand the stages it needs to go through to be successful.

The enterprise lifecycle repeats itself in businesses of all types and sizes. The cycle not only reflects new business start-ups and high growth businesses, but can also be seen when developing internal business ideas in larger organisations. The enterprise lifecycle looks like this:

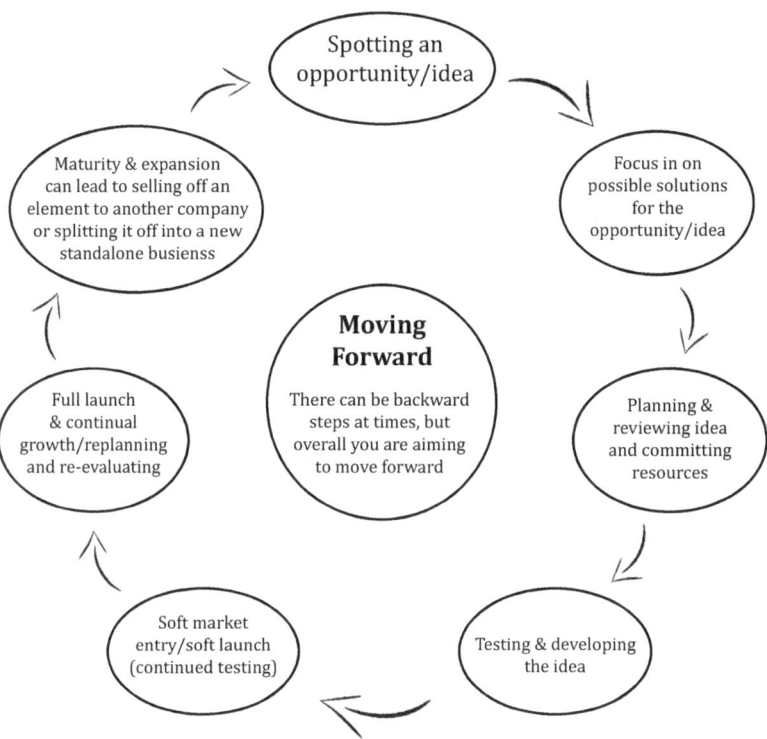

Recognition and rewards

Enterprising staff need to be developing and improving their skills. For many staff members, having the opportunity to develop can be a reward in itself. As their leader and mentor, helping them to develop and value these skills is a valuable element of your work.

Public recognition for work achieved by all involved is really important. This not only provides those involved with a chance to feel the effort was valued and recognised, but also shows other staff members what they could do. Staff can make a profound difference to the direction of the organisation by becoming involved in enterprise projects. Knowing they have helped the organisation be more successful, grow, or just keep staff employed can for some be a great reward.

> ### Case study
>
> When a client asked me to work with their teams to build a more enterprising workforce, they explained that the staff had been told there was a need to reduce the staff numbers if the sales and/or profits didn't improve. Rather than seeing this as a negative, the team agreed to consider ways they could improve the profits and increase the orders—as long as the employers agreed they would keep all the staff on.
>
> A time frame was set and agreed to, and the team worked on developing new ideas—knowing that in doing so, it would ensure their workmates would keep their jobs. At times, they were unsure they could find an idea, but soon they began to realise that speaking to their customers about their needs and how they could help them would be a good starting point.

The new product was launched and the management agreed to keep the staff numbers at the same levels while the idea was rolled out. The team felt proud that they had not only saved jobs, but also that they were continuing to provide their customers with what they wanted.

Staff involved in enterprise projects often talk about how job satisfaction intensifies as they not only find solutions, but have the opportunity to implement them and see the difference they can make. Ultimately, as the staff members develop new skills, new opportunities open up for them to progress within the organisation. Indeed, I believe that this is the right way for staff to progress, rather than the traditional notion that the person who doesn't rock the boat or come up with any ideas getting promoted.

There is evidence that job satisfaction is higher in those individuals whose jobs allow them to take part in more enterprising activities. It's possible that this is about feeling more connected and part of the development and success of the organisation—as much as it's about personal success and financial reward. In addition, we know that staff who feel more job satisfaction are more likely to stay in their job and continue to develop their skills.

Standard rewards rarely work

Before you think financial rewards or bonuses are the right way to get your staff to be more enterprising, think again. Often, this is seen as a quick payment for what could potentially be a long-term gain for the organisation. Think about it this way—if you offer any staff member one day's extra pay for a good idea, does everyone get the same amount? Does it depend on their pay scale? Do more senior staff get a bigger bonus? Should staff just get a treat, extra time off, gift vouchers, or free drinks at the Christmas party? Wow, it's a really difficult one, isn't it?

What if one person's idea saves the organisation thousands and thousands? What if one team member comes up with an idea that sees the organisation go on to make millions? Is one days' pay for the idea fair? Should everyone in their team get the extra money? You could consider % payments, but % of what? Overall organisational increase in profits or % of the income generated from the idea? Some ideas may not actually generate direct revenue. And so the problems continue...

Now think of it this way—you come up with a great idea for the organisation that will help them be stronger in the marketplace and is likely to increase profits. What would you expect to gain from this? As the leader of the organisation, isn't this just your job?

The problem with bonuses is not only are they difficult to work out, but they can have an effect on the rest of the team. Does everyone get a share for example? More than likely, you will need to figure this out amongst your team. If you get this wrong for your workforce the first time, then it's unlikely that they will bother to help you with additional ideas in the future.

For some people, the idea of rewards through promotion, access to new opportunities, and being able to lead a team with their new idea amounts to more freedom to explore opportunities. For many, this can be more important that instant financial reward. In the same way, being offered longer-term benefits such as an increase in overall pay and conditions can be a bigger incentive. This is not only for short-term gain, but longer-term commitment to the organisation.

Financial rewards can be developed where they are suitable within an organisation. These bonuses should be considered carefully to ensure they are aligned with the progress of the project, and the potential income creation for the organisation.

I'm still worried that my staff will leave

Enterprising staff are loyal. They don't wake up each morning thinking about how they can leave the company or how they can take their ideas and make more money for themselves. Instead they are focused on working on their employer's business to improve it and make where they work a better place to be.

However, if you encourage staff to be enterprising and then withdraw your support or make it hard for them to develop their enterprising idea, they may decide to leave. They may decide that it's too frustrating to stay with their employer and take the risk of leaving rather than staying with an unsupportive employer.

If you don't support enterprise, the staff who stay might be the ones who don't actually care about the success of the company. Staff who don't engage in the business or feel part of a team. Are these the type of staff you want to have? Or would you prefer the ones you let leave when you didn't support them in their enterprise activities?

Supporting graduates

Recruiting graduates is often a great way of bringing in new ways of thinking, expertise, and energy to an organisation. Graduates who enter a workplace will often have expectations of being able to use their enterprising ways of thinking. But they soon become frustrated when they are blocked from being enterprising.

For many younger generation employees, it's about having a level of autonomy — being able to work on their own ideas in their own way. To handle this, you may need to alter your management style into one as a guide and mentor rather than an influencer and informer.

Employees as partners

Staff members who are enterprising or who need to be enterprising are likely to face a variety of barriers and have concerns over their role within the organisation. For many, they are likely to be concerned for their own future. They may wonder what will happen to them and their job role moving forward. If their enterprise project is successful, will they still be needed? If their enterprise project fails, will they be asked to leave and seen as unsuccessful? Your role as a manager is to support them and help them manage this situation.

Of course, enterprise offers a huge range of possibilities and this also includes the way in which the enterprise project is rolled out. Projects can be set up as separate businesses and staff may have the opportunity to be involved in these new business units.

If staff have ideas and dreams of going it alone, it may not be the end of the world. It's possible to find alternative working arrangements other than a clear employer / employee relationship. For example, it's possible to run a business together as a collaborative project so that you don't completely lose the staff member or the opportunity of being involved in their idea.

Consider how you engage your staff in enterprise activities rather than bringing in new staff members to take on new enterprising projects. It can be best to avoid making big staffing decisions too soon into the project or bringing in new people who do not connect or engage with the existing team. Try to work with your team to bring them along with you on the journey, rather than forcing changes early on. Work with the skills you have and support them to develop any additional areas where possible.

As an enterprise organisation, your staff are vital to your success. This means you need to support and manage your staff in the right way:

- Ensure your staff are all aware of the bigger picture, the aims of the organisation, why enterprise needs to take place, and their own role in the organisation.
- Develop relationships with your staff based on trust, dependability, and open communication.
- Ensure staff have a shared purpose in developing the organisation and work collaboratively, rather than competitively.
- Allow enterprising staff to use their own initiative and make decisions without checking with you — develop two-way trust.
- Offer support through knowledge and experience sharing and mentoring staff.
- Encourage a culture of personal accountability, not blame.
- When staff make mistakes, work with them to accept their mistakes and learn from them to improve in the future.
- Build reflection time into the essence of your organisation for all staff.
- Manage expectations and keep your staff informed about the business, not in the dark.

- Have a positive attitude towards risk and experimentation and this will follow through to your staff.
- Financial rewards are often short-term. Instead, consider long-term rewards such as promotions, recognition, and opportunities.

Final Words from the Author

However you see your organisation's future, it is likely that you will need to implement changes along the way. These changes may be required to enable your organisation to become more stable, increase income, or generate new ways of working to save money or find new revenue streams. Trying to develop new ideas without involving your employees is likely to lead to projects failing when they do not meet the needs of customers. Staff will feel unwilling or uncommitted to adopting the change and will lack the engagement needed to ensure the organisation learns and grows.

By creating a more enterprising way of working across the whole organisation, it is possible to develop ideas through collaboration and genuine need, leading to a more positive end result. Organisations across the globe will have team members who are always willing to push the envelope and accept that their ideas will ruffle feathers, but they will try anyway. These individuals often become enterprising team members, but only when they are encouraged and supported will they add value to your organisation. You have a choice—encourage, support, and enable them to move their ideas forward or lose them to your competitors. Crush their enterprising mind-sets and discover how much unstructured disruption they can create, or help them flourish into enterprising individuals who can help push your organisation forward.

Staff who are stretchy and embrace enterprise within the organisation are agents for change. Their aim is to improve the organisation, its processes, and its offerings for the benefit of the customers, staff, and the organisation's stability. A revolution is coming and enterprising staff will be a vital part of that change.

Moving Forward...

Now you are at the end of the book, you may feel like you are just beginning your enterprise journey. You may be wondering what should I do next? Well, first go and try some of the things this book has shown you. Then, if you still feel like doing more, you should consider the following options:

- Share it with your team
- Work with Rebecca in-house
- Book Rebecca to speak at an event
- Take one of Rebecca's online programs

Work with Rebecca Jones – in house

Rebecca inspires organisations, their leaders, managers, and staff to embrace enterprise within their business and understand how it cannot only benefit the organisation, but also their end customers. She runs in-house masterclasses, workshops, and residential programs.

Rebecca can help you achieve:

- increased profitability
- more sustainable ways of working
- better customer service
- improved staff engagement
- higher staff retention.

Book Rebecca to speak at an event

Looking for an engaging business speaker for your event or conference that the audience will enjoy listening to, connect with, and learn from? Rebecca is a well-known international speaker and will deliver a truly positive, up-beat, and memorable presentation for your business conference or meeting. Rebecca will inspire your audience to achieve more, improve their mind-set, and develop more successful businesses. Rebecca will share stories and experiences as well as evidence-based knowledge on how to develop and grow as individuals, employees, and business owners.

Speaking from the heart, Rebecca has the ability to engage with any audience from school leavers to Chief Executives, self-employed to professional-level staff. Her thought-provoking and often funny stories demonstrate how we are sometimes our own worst enemies and how to shift your mind-set to achieve more. Her talks provide solutions that anyone can immediately transfer into their own lives, work, or business.

As an inspirational business speaker, Rebecca can provide you with messages around personal development, mind-set, enterprise, innovation staff engagement, customer-focused businesses, and organisational growth.

If you would like to discuss booking Rebecca to speak at an event or run a workshop, please visit www.rebeccajones.biz.

Take a look at Rebecca's online resources

Rebecca regularly runs webinars and offers online learning solutions. To discover more, visit www.rebeccajones.biz.

Further reading

Argote, L. & Ingram, P. (2000) Knowledge transfer: A basis for competitive advantage in firms.

Bosma, N. et al. (2010) Intrapreneurship and international study. Zoetermeer, Scientific Analysis of Entrepreneurship and SME's (SCALES)

Desouza, K.C. (1979) Intrapreneurship: Managing ideas within your organisation. University of Toronto Press, Toronto

Dweck, C, Dr (2012) Mind-set- How you can fulfill your potential. London, Constable & Robinson.

Gartner, WB (1988) "Who is an entrepreneur?" Is the wrong question, American journal of small business, 12, 4:11-32

Haller, H. E. (2014) Intrapreneurship: Ignite Innovation. Silver Eagle press, Idaho

Histich R.D. (2012) Corporate Entrepreneurship. McGraw Hill, New York

Kanter, R. (1988) When a thousand flowers bloom: Structural, collective and social conditions for innovation in organisations, Research in organisational behaviour, (Vol. 10) pp169 – 211

Kolb, D. A. (1984). Experiential learning: Experience as the source of learning and development (Vol. 1). Englewood Cliffs, NJ: Prentice-Hall.

Lumpkin, G.T. & Dess, G.G. (1996) Clarifying the entrepreneurial orientation construct and linking it to performance. Academy of management review, 21, 1: 135-172

MacLeod, D. & Clarke, A. (2009) Engaging for Success: enhancing performance through employee engagement. Report for Dept for Business UK government.

Oden, H. W. (1997) Managing Corporate Culture, Innovation and Intraprenuership. Quorium Books

Pinchot, G. (1984) Who is the Intrapreneur? In: Intrapreneuring: Why You Don't Have to Leave the Corporation to Become an Entrepreneur. New York: Harper & Row.

Pinchot, G. (1985) Intrapreneuring, Harper & Row, New York

Shane, S. (2003) A General Theory of Entrepreneurship: The Individual-opportunity Nexus. Edward Elgar Publishing, London

Senge, P. (1990) The Fifth Discipline: The Art and Practice of The Learning Organization. Random House, London

Syed, M. (2010) Bounce: The myth of talent and the power of practice. HarperCollins, London